FIFTY HOMILIES
FROM THE
DEACON'S DESK

KATE,
GOD BLESS YOU AND
YOUR FAMILY — MAY
YOU FEEL GOD's LOVE ALWAYS!

DEACON RICK WAGNER

ISBN 978-1-68197-951-9 (Paperback)
ISBN 978-1-68197-952-6 (Digital)

Christian Faith Publishing, Inc.
296 Chestnut Street
Meadville, PA 16335
www.christianfaithpublishing.com

Printed in the United States of America

ADVENT

BE VIGILANT AT ALL TIMES

First Sunday of Advent 2012   *Jeremiah 33:14-16*
1 Thessalonians 3:12-4:2
Luke 21:25-28, 34-36

When I am preparing to preach, I read the Scripture passages over and over again, seeing what word or phrase or expression might jump out at me. In Luke's gospel today, it was the phrase "Be vigilant at all times."

The gospels are full of such warnings: be vigilant, be awake and alert, be prepared, be watchful.

Those who lived during the several generations following the death of Jesus knew what it meant to be vigilant. They thought that the Second Coming would soon be upon them, and they wanted to be ready. They believed, so they were watchful and alert and vigilant. To many of us living today, people who practice that type of vigilance would be considered paranoid.

Society's lack of faith has made us less vigilant. Because we are not vigilant, because we are not alert and prepared, we leave the door open to temptation and sin.

If we truly believed what we say in the Nicene Creed, that "He will come again in glory to judge the living and the dead," wouldn't we be better prepared? Wouldn't we be doing the right thing all the time, just in case today was the day?

What state would Christ find us in if His return in glory happened to be today? How prepared are we to be judged?

I began reflecting on how much time we spend preparing for other things. Our favorite music group is coming to town for a concert. We buy tickets six months in advance. We call friends, plan, and make arrangements. When the event is a week away, we touch base with everyone to confirm plans. Finally, the day of the event comes. We only work a half day so we can get home, change our clothes, and go out to dinner with enough time to get in line and be in our seats when the concert starts.

We show incredible vigilance in our pursuit of musical enter-tainment.

What planning and preparation have we done to welcome Jesus into our lives? Why are we less vigilant when it comes to our faith?

Every spring, young men plan elaborate ways to ask young ladies to go to the prom with them. They parachute into backyards or spell out the word *prom* in rose petals or hide in lockers wearing gorilla suits. They spend (or their parents spend) hundreds of dollars on tux rental and prom dresses. Young ladies spend hours fixing their hair and putting on their makeup. The couple has their picture taken before climbing into limousines. They spend Saturday night dancing and looking good.

They show incredible vigilance in their pursuit of the perfect date.

We spend a great deal of time planning and preparing and fussing over things of this world. My point is not that we should not go to concerts or proms, but that we should show at least the same degree of care in preparing for the coming of Jesus Christ.

Advent has become the number of shopping days till Christmas.

I had an opportunity to go to Haiti two years ago. It was just over a year after the major earthquake that devastated what was already a Third World country. We landed in Port-au-Prince and drove through the city. Thousands upon thousands of Haitians still lived in rubble. The destruction and the smell and the poverty and the absolute desolation were like nothing I had ever experienced.

We drove the winding dirt road up into the mountains to the Catholic church we would be serving. We stayed in a square concrete block structure with a sheet of metal serving as the roof and slept in sleeping bags on the floor. This was the church rectory.

Each day we would go out and visit with one of the nine satellite chapels up in the mountains. We brought medicine, rosaries, and human contact to the Haitians living in the areas surrounding each chapel.

One day, Fr. Calique was able to go with us. He was the one priest who served the main church and all nine chapels. That day we were going to Our Lady of Mount Carmel Chapel, the most remote chapel, way up into the mountains. It was not possible to drive as the path was too narrow and dangerous.

So this must be the day they warned me about. I had been told that on one of the days we would be taking a hike that might be "a bit of a challenge."

I learned that it was three hours away on foot, and I swear it was uphill both ways. It was the most physically demanding thing I have ever done. I was humbled at one point when I needed to sit down on a rock at the side of the mountainous path to catch my breath. While gasping for air, an elderly Haitian man with a cane walked past me and smiled and waved.

When we arrived at the chapel, Fr. Calique asked someone to start ringing the chapel bell. We were told that the bell was the signal to the people in the area that Mass would begin in two hours. It was not possible for a priest to have a regular Mass schedule, so they used the bell to let folks know a priest was present and Mass would be celebrated in the chapel. Some would need to travel on foot nearly two hours to get there in time.

The chapel had been crippled by the earthquake. One wall was completely gone. Parts of the other three walls were missing, and large cracks were everywhere. The building looked like it could collapse any minute. Boards supported by concrete blocks served as pews.

But in the sweltering heat on this Tuesday afternoon at one o'clock, the chapel was standing room only. Men in buttoned up shirts and hats, women and girls in their nicest dresses. A big smile on every face. They sang and they prayed with true joy in their hearts.

We sat in the back and watched when the collection basket was passed. I saw work-worn fingers pull small coins from tattered change purses. I had tears in my eyes when the basket arrived at our seats, and I saw what amounted to around 75 cents lying in the basket.

"For the rich gave from their surplus wealth, but the poor widow, from her poverty, has contributed all she had, her whole livelihood" (Mark 12:44).

When the chapel bell rang, these people dropped whatever they were doing and answered the call. Whether they were digging in the rocky soil to try to grow food for their family or fortifying the walls of their concrete block home or carrying water up a mountain on their heads—when that bell rang, they were prepared.

They were alert and ready to respond. I learned many things during my week in Haiti. But one thing the Haitian people taught me was the meaning of the phrase "be vigilant at all times."

—December 2012

PRAY ALWAYS WITH JOY

Second Sunday of Advent 2012   *Baruch 5:1-9*
                                   Philippians 1:4-6, 8-11
                                   Luke 3:1-6

This time of year there is much talk of gift giving and finding someone that perfect gift. What better gift-giving message could there be than the one we hear in Paul's Letter to the Philippians today? He tells the community, "I pray always with joy in my every prayer for all of you."

Can you imagine a better gift?

Think about how awesome this would be—someone not only praying for me, but also *praying always with joy.*

What if we did this? What if all of us prayed always with joy for one another?

All our prayers for others and all our prayers with joy.

I often have people ask me to pray for them or for their needs, and I do. I add them to my prayer list. Paul makes me wonder if I am being too mechanical.

Am I just going through the motions when I pray for those people? Do I pray with joy always? What would it be like if I did? What would it be like if we *all* did?

⸺⸺⸺

I had the honor of attending the installation of Archbishop Tobin last Monday. It was a powerful service, a beautiful Mass with beautiful music. It was almost overwhelming. The best part was the full participation of everyone in attendance. Everyone responded to all the prayers and sang all the hymns.

Everyone participated in full voice. The sound shook the walls of the cathedral. Our prayer came alive. We were praying with joy.

What if all of us responded like this every time we attended Mass? Do we need to be in the cathedral to do that? Do we need to install an archbishop to have this type of participation? Was Jesus any more present at that service than He is at our weekend Mass? What would it sound like to shake the walls of St. Pius X with our prayer? Isn't *that* what Paul means when he speaks of praying joyfully?

⸺⸺⸺

I watch the students at my school as they process to the altar to receive Holy Communion. I see distracted teens gazing at something else. I hear mumbled responses when I offer the Body or Blood of Christ.

Then a young person will step forward, standing upright and reverent, hands extended, eyes locked on me, and my favorite part—a smile on his or her face.

How can you not smile, knowing that you are receiving Jesus? How could you not be in awe?

I say, "Body of Christ," and this young person says, "Amen" with true conviction. An amen that says, "Yes, I believe that this is the Body of Christ. I would stake my life on it!"

What if we all received Holy Communion like this? Joyfully and with conviction, rather than as part of some methodical routine? Isn't *that* what Paul means when he speaks of praying joyfully?

—————

For the young people here today: When a parent asks you, or tells you, to do something like clean your room, cut the grass, or clear the dinner dishes, how do you respond?

There are times when you want to say, "No" or "I don't want to," but you know it would not be a good idea to say that out loud. You really don't have time to do it. You don't want to do it. You are irritated that Mom even asked you to do it.

You do it, but you complain or you're grumpy or you rush through it just to get it done. The work gets done, but it is certainly not done with joy.

Even though I use children in my example, it doesn't let the adults off the hook. How do *we* respond when our boss or our spouse ask us to do something? How about when a friend asks a favor of us? How much joy is in our efforts? How much joy is in our hearts?

What if, when we helped one another, we did it from a place of love? Isn't *that* what Paul means when he speaks of praying joyfully?

—————

During Advent, maybe we should be thinking about what kind of gift to give to God. What do you get for the Man who has everything?

Maybe our gift to God should be joy. Participating fully at Mass … with joy. Receiving the Body and Blood of Christ … with joy. Being in service to others … with joy. Or as Paul suggests, "Praying always with joy in our every prayer."

When Paul writes of praying, he doesn't mean words alone; he is talking about living a prayerful life. Prayer is reciting the Our Father, and it is also visiting the elderly in nursing homes. Prayer is an hour of Adoration, and it is also an hour serving at the soup kitchen. Prayer is saying the rosary, and it is also putting aside your computer to shoot some baskets with your children. Prayer is coming to Mass a few minutes early to sit in silence; it is also taking your spouse's hand and giving it a reassuring squeeze.

The greatest gift we can give to God is to live our entire lives as one joyful prayer. Isn't *that* what Paul means when he speaks of praying joyfully?

—December 2012

WHAT MAIL?

Second Sunday of Advent 2013   *Isaiah 11:1-10*
                                                  Romans 15:4-9
                                                  Matthew 3:1-12

When I was young, I used to read a comic strip in the Sunday paper called "Family Circus." At the time, I didn't think it was all that funny. It didn't make much sense to me. It wasn't until I was older and was married and had a family that I found the humor in this comic. It all made sense then.

One of the recurring story lines in the comic had to do with how distracted children can get when carrying out the simplest of tasks. For example, in the first scene of the comic, the dad would say something like, "Billy, could you go out and get the mail?" The mailbox was just one hundred feet from the front door.

The second scene showed Billy walking into the house thirty minutes later empty-handed, and Dad asking, "Where's the mail?" To which Billy responds with a confused look on his face, "What mail?"

The final, large scene had a dotted line indicating Billy's somewhat indirect route to the mailbox: He stopped to pet the dog. He ran back and forth through the sprinkler a few times. He jumped over the fence and sat on the porch with his neighbor and enjoyed some lemonade and a cookie. He ran across the street to check out his friend's new tree house. He pushed himself along the sidewalk on a skateboard. He stopped to get a push-up from the ice cream truck. And finally, after mastering the hopscotch course on the sidewalk, he headed inside.

Instead of taking a straight path to complete the task, he had hopped, skipped, and jumped into a multitude of distractions. If I didn't have a son like this myself, I would never have believed it.

Billy knew where the mailbox was and understood the task he needed to complete, but he allowed distractions to take him off course.

Today's gospel tells *us* to go get the mail: *prepare the way of the Lord, make straight his paths.*

We understand the way of the Lord, we know the path that will take us to Him, but we allow distractions to take us off course. Somehow, on our way down the path, our priorities get out of whack. We put off what we know is right until another day, thinking we have all the time in the world. After all, the mail will still be there, won't it?

Therein lies our problem: our human need for immediate gratification.

The dog was right there, so Billy petted him. The sprinkler felt good, so he ran through it a few times. Tree climbing and skateboarding were fun and immediate. Billy was hungry, and a cookie and a push-up were readily accessible. When it was all said and done, because of the distractions, he never made it to the mailbox.

Luckily, it was only mail he was after.

Today's gospel, actually the entire Advent season, encourages us to take the path of least distraction. We want eternal life and know it is in the mailbox at the end of the path. If we have heeded the advice of Isaiah and John the Baptist, that path will be straight, and our journey, uncorrupted by distractions.

If we are easily distracted, maybe we should turn the tables on our way of thinking. Maybe we should allow ourselves to be *distracted by God.*

Let's pretend for a moment that our ultimate goal is to accumulate and immerse ourselves in earthly things, things of no real value. So all those earthly things are in that mailbox, and I'm on my way down the path to retrieve them.

But I get distracted by prayer. It is immediate, and I get a rush from having this intimate conversation with God.

Before I can get back on the path to my ultimate goal of earthly things, I get distracted again, this time by reconciliation. It feels so good to be cleansed and renewed and unburdened by sin. I actually feel lighter.

The mailbox is still there, but I get distracted again by Mass on the other side of the fence. I sit with my neighbor and am nourished by the Word, by the Eucharist, by being part of the body of Christ, by being part of something bigger than myself.

I take the long way around toward the mailbox but am distracted again. Right across the street are opportunities to serve others. I am drawn to them. I see the look of joy on the faces of those I serve. I feel their gratitude. I listen to their stories and hear the sound of new-found hope in their voices. I find myself more and more distracted by service. It becomes immediate gratification for me.

Other distractions flood my senses, keeping me from my mailbox full of earthly things. The dotted line of my path to the mailbox showed that I veered off-course to try fasting, to participate in a Bible study, to visit someone in prison, and to comfort a friend.

All of these distractions!

Like Billy, I never made it to my mailbox full of earthly things. I was so distracted by God that I never made it.

I will leave you with three possible paths:

1. Not recommended: We can take the route that Billy took and allow earthly things to distract us from the opportunity to get the mail—to achieve salvation.

2. We can take our chances, continuing our pursuit of earthly things, and *hope* that we will be distracted by God.

3. Or, the preferred option: We can heed the warnings of Isaiah and John the Baptist and make straight our path to salvation.

We can take it seriously and, when we head to the mailbox, not allow ourselves to get distracted by the things of this earth.

We can treat it like it is the last opportunity we'll ever have to retrieve our mail because it just may be.

—December 2013

GOD, WHAT ARE YOU WAITING FOR?

Third Sunday of Advent 2014   *Isaiah 61:1-2A, 10-11*
                                                            1 Thessalonians 5:16-24
                                                            John 1:6-8, 19-28

It is fitting that during the Advent season, during this time of preparation, we hear the voices of Isaiah, Paul, and John the Baptist.

Isaiah brought "glad tidings to the poor" and foretold of a time when the Lord God will "make justice and peace spring up before all the nations."

Help is on the way.

It was also Isaiah who prophesied about a voice of one crying out in the desert. We know now that the voice to which he was referring was that of John the Baptist. John's entire message was that of preparation for the One who was to come after him, the One whose sandal strap he was not worthy to untie. He called the people to make straight the path. John was there to "testify to the light."

Help is on the way.

Paul's Letter to the Thessalonians, another voice crying out, was also about preparation: Pray without ceasing. In all circumstances give thanks. Refrain from every kind of evil. He echoed John the Baptist's call to make straight the path.

Help is on the way.

These voices are crying out to us to be prepared. We prepare for the day Isaiah spoke of when he said: "As the earth brings forth its plants, and a garden makes its growth spring up, so will the Lord God make justice and praise spring up before all the nations."

With all that is going on in this world, "justice and praise springing up before all the nations" sounds pretty good.

I don't normally challenge God, but when I studied this passage I thought, "We get it, *help is on the way.* But it's 2014. Isaiah said this 2,800 years ago. God, what are You waiting for?"

———

I remember having a meeting with my administrative assistant, Cathy, several years ago. We met each week to look ahead on the school calendar and talk through all the work that needed to be done to prepare for upcoming events.

The calendar was loaded, so for that particular meeting, there was a long list of things to do. I remember reading through the list we had compiled and saying something like this to Cathy: "I need to get a memo out to the teachers about next week. I need to contact the grade school principals and get their input. I need to confirm that the gym is reserved for the assembly. I need to set a meeting with the department chairs." And I looked at Cathy and added, "And of course when I say 'I', I mean *you.*"

———

Back to my challenge: God, what are you waiting for? Why is justice and praise not springing up yet? God might well respond: "I will make justice and praise spring up before all the nations." And He will look at me and add, "And of course when I say 'I', I mean *you.*"

What's God waiting for? He's waiting for *us!*

He is waiting for us to commit. We are part of God's team and He needs all of us, *expects* all of us, to join in His work.

The thought of helping with God's work is intimidating. It is especially intimidating if you operate under the assumption that God is up there and we're down here working in isolation.

But that is not the case. John the Baptist tells us, "There is one among you that you do not recognize."

If we recognize that Jesus is right here with us, working with us side by side, it should not be intimidating at all. It should be energizing.

So what does committing to God's work look like? Where do we begin? Maybe we begin with the words of St. Paul in his Letter to the Thessalonians: "Pray without ceasing."

That is certainly a lofty and admirable goal, but not very practical. It is not practical, not even possible, if we only think of prayer in the traditional sense—kneel down, fold our hands, and recite words of prayer committed to memory back in grade school. We can't do that without ceasing, or at least I know I can't.

So we must expand our definition of prayer to include living a prayerful life. What we can do is live life with a prayerful disposition, with a prayerful spirit.

In this week's edition of *The Criterion* newspaper, Archbishop Tobin offered four suggestions on preparing for Christmas that speak to the idea of living a prayerful life:

- Set quiet time aside for prayer – I may not be able to pray without ceasing, but I can spare a few minutes of alone time with God.
- Go to confession – wipe the slate clean and start anew, filled with God's grace. In Fr. Jim's letter in the bulletin – he lists several opportunities to go to confession over the next week.

- Be more faithful, and attentive, to our Mass attendance. Mass is a beautiful reminder that God is with us. It allows us to better recognize His presence in our lives.
- Give spiritual gifts – a smile, a kind word, or a helping hand to those in need.

God wants us to seek Him out. He wants us to engage with Him, to maintain an ongoing dialogue. What we do in our daily lives should be about Him and for Him, about others and for others.

I can't kneel, fold my hands, and recite words of prayer without ceasing, but I *can* live a life that glorifies God. I can seek Him out and be about His business.

Today's readings are not included in the Advent season by chance. They speak to what Advent calls us to do—prepare the way of the Lord.

Do His work. Seek Him out. Be about His business. In so doing, we will have prepared the way for Him. God feels welcomed in such a world; He feels invited.

Help is on the way.

—December 2014

Using the Gravy Boat

First Sunday of Advent 2015 *Jeremiah 33:14-16*
1 Thessalonians 3:12-4:2
Luke 21:25-28, 34-36

Advent is here. Thanksgiving has come and gone. We have survived Black Friday. We start the Advent season with joyful anticipation of Christmas and the arrival of the infant Jesus. Perhaps on your way to church this morning you were wondering what uplifting readings would be used to kick off the Advent season. What words of hopeful promise would be shared and reflected upon?

As I began reading the gospel, you probably leaned forward in the pew, ready to smile and feel the love. What words of joy do you have for us, Jesus?

Then we heard the Gospel of Luke, wherein Jesus said to his disciples: "There will be signs ... People will die of fright in anticipation of what is coming upon the world, for the powers of the heavens will be shaken. For that day will assault everyone who lives on the face of the earth ... pray that you have the strength to escape the tribulations that are imminent ... that day will catch you by surprise like a trap."

Okay. Happy Advent!

So why was *this* gospel chosen for the first Sunday of Advent?

It is important to understand that the liturgical season of Advent has a two-fold purpose. Most of us think of Advent only in terms of how it relates to Christmas, as a time of preparation and anticipation of the Nativity of Jesus.

Advent is also intended to direct the mind and heart to await Christ's *Second* Coming. The Second Coming is described as Jesus returning to earth once again, not as an infant, but rather as a powerful king.

From Luke's gospel: "And then they will see the Son of Man coming in a cloud with power and great glory."

Jesus will return to set things right in a world that has turned its back on Him. Some understand the Second Coming to mean their own death, when they will meet Jesus face-to-face. Either way, we have no timeline for the event.

We know that Christmas will come on December 25, so it's easy to prepare for *that* day. However, Christ's Second Coming is a different story; we don't know when this will occur.

How do we prepare for *that*?

—————

We can discuss the two-fold purpose of the Advent season in terms of cleaning our house, or "getting our house in order."

When we are going to entertain guests in our home, Carol puts me to work. The house gets cleaned from top to bottom. Bathrooms must shine. The "good dishes" and fancy serving trays are brought out, and the gravy boat makes a rare appearance.

Newly purchased things suddenly appear in our home: a new rug for the entryway, candles placed in several strategic locations, a pillow tilted just so on the couch, and so on.

The practical side of me says, "Won't our guests accept us as we are?

"Our house *never* looks like this. Are we trying to fool them?"

But the more intuitive side of me, the side of me that responds to Carol's orders to clean, knows that by spending time preparing our home, we are showing our guests that we consider their visit to be important. We anticipate the time of their arrival and we prepare our home to welcome them.

This example of getting our house in order is similar to our preparation for the birth of Jesus at Christmas. It is important to us and worthy of the time and effort we spend preparing for it. So we use the weeks leading up to Christmas to be more intentional in our prayer life, to go to confession, to reflect on the many gifts God has given us, and to reach out in service to others.

We get our house in order so Jesus knows His arrival is important to us.

⸺ꝏꝏ⸺

When we were kids, my parents were occasionally brave enough to leave us home without a babysitter. As they were heading out for the evening, they would share their expectations of us and tell us what time they were going to be home.

We would wait until the car pulled out of the driveway. Once it was clear that they were gone, chaos ensued. We jumped on the couch, climbed on the counter, and pulled out all the snacks Mom had hidden in the top cabinets, played tackle football in the house, chased each other, and built forts out of furniture. All rules went out the window.

Then about fifteen minutes before our parents were scheduled to return, the oldest sibling would announce that it was time to put the house in order. We ran around, put cushions back on couches, took the football to the garage, returned furniture to its rightful place, and swept up the crumbs from the forbidden snacks.

We would take one last look around and would be sitting angelically on the couch, watching TV, when our parents returned home. We knew when they were coming home, so we anticipated and prepared for their arrival.

However, inevitably the day came when our parents returned home unexpectedly.

Their plans had fallen through, and they came home early to find us in mid-chaos.

—◦◦◦◦◦◦◦—

Listen again to the words of Jesus in today's gospel. He was describing the look in my dad's eyes when he saw the condition of his home: "People will die of fright in anticipation of what is coming upon the world … pray that you have the strength to escape the tribulations that are imminent … and that day will catch you by surprise like a trap."

—◦◦◦◦◦◦◦—

This is the second purpose of the Advent season—preparing for the Second Coming of Christ. Preparing for the unknown, with no definitive day or timeline to guide you, and unsure of exactly what the Second Coming will mean for you.

After describing the fright and tribulation of being caught unprepared, Jesus gave His disciples this advice: "Be vigilant at all times."

You don't know when to be prepared? *Always* be prepared.

Do what you know is right, even when no one is looking. That might mean leaving the snacks in the top cabinet, the football in the garage, and furniture where it belongs.

Always be prepared.

In today's second reading, St. Paul shared similar advice. He encouraged the Thessalonians to get their houses in order. He wrote, "We gave you the instructions that we received from Jesus. You know how you should conduct yourselves to please God. May the Lord make you increase and abound in love for one another and for all … so that you will be blameless at the coming of our Lord."

We look forward with joyous anticipation of the coming of Jesus at Christmas, so we work hard to be prepared for His arrival. Advent calls us to this preparation.

However, it is important that we not limit our preparation to the four weeks leading up to Christmas. What are we doing the rest of the year to prepare for the Second Coming and our own face-to-face meeting with Jesus? We must be vigilant at all times.

Get your house in order because it's the right thing to do. *Keep* it in order because you never know when Dad is coming home.

—November 2015

GOD STUFF!

Fourth Sunday of Advent 2015   *Micah 5:1-4A*
                                                Hebrews 10:5-10
                                                Luke 1:39-45

With the Christmas season approaching, I thought I would take a moment to reflect on the practice of exchanging gifts. I will focus primarily on the *receiving* of gifts, more specifically, how one *responds* to receiving a gift.

Allow me to offer three examples from the wide range of possible responses.

Example #1: After school one day, five students and I spent three hours in the rain, raking leaves for my elderly neighbor. We filled up sixty-four large trash bags with the leaves from her front yard. Darkness set in, and as we were putting away the rakes and leaf blower, my neighbor stepped out onto her front porch and called me over.

What was her response to this gift we had given her? Her response was, and I quote, "Aren't you going to do the backyard?"

Our gift was not enough. She wasn't satisfied; she wanted more.

Example #2: There is a seven-second video on YouTube that is very popular right now. The premise is that a little boy gives the very same response for every single gift he receives. So for fun, his parents wrapped up an avocado and added it to his pile of Christmas gifts.

The boy worked through the pile. When it came time to open this fake gift, the polite young boy tore off the paper, smiled, and said, "An avocado! Thanks!"

He then dropped the avocado and grabbed the next present. What that response offered in politeness, it lacked in sincerity. He may or may not have liked the gift. He may or may not have been grateful to the person who gave him the gift. He simply went through the motions.

He was a creature of habit when it came to opening gifts.

Example #3: In 1997, there was a movie starring Jim Carrey called *Liar Liar*. It was the story of an absentee father trying his best to reconnect with his son. He gave a gift to his son on his birthday—a ball, mitt, and baseball cap. When the boy opened it, his eyes lit up, and he said enthusiastically, "Baseball stuff!"

He then thanked his dad profusely. Once he got over the excitement of receiving this awesome gift, he asked his dad to go outside and play catch with him. It was something the boy really wanted. His excitement and gratitude were genuine.

He didn't even need to say, "Thank you" to his dad—his reaction said it all. To top it off, the first thing he wanted to do with his gift was share it with someone else.

———

Today's readings address how we respond to God's gifts. When He presents us with a gift, what do we offer in return? What are His expectations of us? What do you give to the Man who has everything?

In the second reading, it is clear what God *does not* want in return. In the Letter to the Hebrews, we heard, "Sacrifices and offerings (are) neither desired nor delighted in."

For thousands of years, sacrifice of animals and burnt offerings were a worshipper's go-to gift for God. Yet we hear today that those things were of no use to Him.

God gives us gifts each day:

- The gift of life
- The gift of another day
- The beauty found in nature
- People in our lives who love us
- The reassuring hug of a friend
- The warmth that comes from serving others
- The peace that comes from knowing God as a friend and companion

These gifts, and many more, are poured out for us daily, if we are open to receiving them.

How do *we* respond to the gifts God has given us? Do we respond like my neighbor? Do we miss out on the gift right in front of us because we are already anticipating the next gift? Are we never satisfied?

When God presents us with a gift, is our response, "This isn't what I wanted"?

Or maybe we are just going through the motions, like the avocado kid. Do we give lip service by offering a word of thanks and then throw God's gift on the pile with the rest? Do we take His gifts for granted? I know God will be here tomorrow, offering me gifts again; maybe I'll thank him then.

God does not want empty gestures or well-rehearsed responses any more than He wants burnt offerings. He wants genuine gratitude. When He gives us a gift, He wants us to accept it with the same love with which it was given; He wants us to *value* His gifts.

God does not need us to yell out "God stuff!" with enthusiasm each time we recognize and receive a gift He has given us. However, He does want us to carry that type of excitement in our hearts.

The beauty of exchanging gifts with God is that our gift does not need to be wrapped up and handed to Him. Our gift to Him is our *response* to His gifts.

To honor God and show our sincere gratitude to Him for the gifts He has given us, we must first recognize them as gifts. Then, we must be open to receiving the gifts, accepting them lovingly. We must embrace the uniqueness of His gift; after all, God's gifts are personal. Finally, we must share the gifts with the world.

That is exactly how Mary, the Mother of God, received the gift given to *her*. She is the ultimate example of one who understood how precious it was to receive a gift from God and responded accordingly.

Can you even imagine what Mary must have been thinking, how she must have felt, when the angel appeared to her and revealed the gift she was receiving from God? A thirteen or fourteen-year-old girl, being told that she had been chosen to carry and give birth to the Christ child?

She could have rejected this gift. She could have given the angel any number of excuses: "It's too overwhelming. I'm not prepared. I'm too young for such a responsibility. Choose someone else."

But she did not. Instead, Mary honored God by showing sincere gratitude. She recognized that being chosen for this responsibility was a gift. She was open to the gift and accepted it lovingly, which took incredible faith. She believed what she was told and embraced the unique gift.

"Blessed are you who believed that what was spoken to you," her cousin Elizabeth told her. Finally, she shared this gift with the world. Knowing the heartache it would ultimately bring her, she still shared this gift by sending Jesus out into the world to do His work. I came across this passage from 1 Peter recently: "As each one has received a gift, use it to serve one another as good stewards of God's varied grace."

That is how God wants us to respond. *That* is God stuff.

—December 2015

CHRISTMAS

LEFT AT THE TRUCK STOP

Feast of the Holy Family 2012   *Sirach 3:2-6, 12-14*
                                      Colossians 3:12-21
                                      Luke 2:41-52

Young Jesus and I have something in common. In my youth, I too experienced being left behind.

However, when comparing my experience to that of Jesus, the similarities end there:

- Jesus and His parents were part of a caravan traveling home after Passover. We were heading to Wisconsin for vacation.
- Jesus chose to stay behind. My parents forgot me.
- Jesus spent his time in the temple. I was left at a truck stop on I-94.
- When Jesus' parents found Him, He was sitting among the Rabbis, demonstrating his deep understanding of theology. When my parents found me, I was chatting with a truck driver, wearing a cowboy hat, and sucking on a popsicle.
- When Jesus saw his parents, He said, "Why were you looking for me?" When I saw my parents, I started crying.

Some gospel passages have so many life-giving messages to offer that it becomes difficult to determine exactly which one to focus on. Today we have that type of reading.

Should our focus be on twelve-year-old Jesus and the astonishing knowledge and understanding he was demonstrating in the temple? Or is the message more reflective in nature?

Perhaps the gospel is asking us, "Do you notice when Jesus is missing from your life? And if so, do you go looking for Him?'

Maybe the Church is calling us home with a subtle message: If you are having difficulty finding Jesus, you should know that you can always find him here … in His Father's house.

———

Since this gospel passage was chosen as the reading for the Feast of the Holy Family, I believe today we are being directed to concentrate on the dynamics of the family unit and its connection to our faith.

Certainly all of us who are parents can relate to what Mary and Joseph must have felt throughout this ordeal. I won't ask for a show of hands, but I'm sure most of you parents, if not all, know the feeling of your heart dropping into your stomach when you realize that you do not know where your child is.

At the state fair, parents look at each other with panic when they realize that their four-year-old is not with them. Mom says, "I thought he was with you." And Dad responds, "I thought he was with *you*."

A father paces the floor at 12:30 at night, staring at the clock. His daughter's curfew is midnight, but she isn't home, and she doesn't answer her phone.

We can feel the heartfelt intensity of Mary's simple words to Jesus: "Son, why have you done this to us? Your father and I have been looking for you with great anxiety."

It is important to acknowledge that the great anxiety felt by Mary and Joseph was not debilitating. It called them to action. It fueled the search for their son.

There are other times in the lives of parents when they must deal with a child who is lost, if not physically, in some other way. Perhaps the child is lost spiritually. Despite the parents' best intentions, the child's faith is fading or gone altogether. We bring them to Mass, we share our value system with them, we try to inspire them with our own love of the church; but for them, something is missing. They are searching for something else, wanting to discover God in their own time and on their own terms.

We want to bring them home. We want to pull them back in but don't know how without pushing them away. Mary's words echo, "Your father and I have been looking for you with great anxiety."

Sometimes the *relationship* between parents and their children gets lost somewhere along the way. The children don't think they need their parents any more. Priorities come into question. Phone calls and visits become less and less frequent. An unresolved argument that started one day festers until communication is broken off all together.

Both parent and child are hurt that the other has not reached out. Whose fault it is becomes more important than the relationship itself. Only a part of Mary's words remain true. There is certainly great anxiety, but the "looking for you" is gone.

Today we celebrate the Feast of the Holy Family. When the two parents are saints, and the child they are raising is God, it is not a huge leap to be a holy family. However, I think that what is being celebrated on this feast day goes beyond Jesus, Mary, and Joseph to the holiness of the family unit itself.

Children are a gift from God. Parents are entrusted with their care. There is much that goes into caring for a family. Parents nurture their children. They educate them and form them in the faith. They show their love for their children by providing them, to the best of their ability, with food, clothing and shelter, and the other necessities of life.

To be a *holy* family, we must go beyond these minimum expectations. A holy family is one whose members live their lives in service to God and one another. What makes Mary and Joseph shining examples of a holy family was their willingness to look for one another with great anxiety—to recognize that a family member was lost, harness the energy of that anxiety, look for the family member, and bring him home.

When we think of family in *those* terms, we realize that a family is not always made up of a mother, father, and child. That same accountability for one another extends beyond our immediate, traditional families.

If we believe that a holy family is one whose members live their lives in service to God and one another, then your group of friends can be a holy family, caring for one another and providing support when one friend is struggling. The people you work with at the office who notice when you are lost and work with great anxiety to bring you back, or the neighbors who live on your street can be a holy family. This parish community is a holy family.

As every gospel passage reveals in some way, it always come back to one simple message: love God with all your heart and love others as yourself.

I have no proof of this since it is not included in the gospel story. But when Mary and Joseph saw Jesus, despite the fact they were astonished and despite their great anxiety, and *before* they chastised him, I bet they ran to him and wrapped him in a huge hug and told him that they loved him.

Just as the father does when his daughter walks in an hour after curfew.

Just as my Mom and Dad did when they found me in the truck stop on I-94.

—December 2012

FAITH AND SIMPLICITY

Feast of the Holy Family 2013   *Sirach 3:2-6, 12-14*
                                   Colossians 3:12-21
                                   Matthew 2:13-15, 19-23

In our first reading today, we heard from every father's favorite prophet, Sirach. I might suggest that dads make posters of some of the passages from Sirach and post them throughout the house or mail them off to their grown children.

Passages such as:

- Whoever reveres his father will live a long life.
- Take care of your father when he is old.
- Even if your father's mind fails, be considerate of him.
- Kindness to a father will not be forgotten.

I will preach on these important topics from Sirach with my own children at a later date. For now, I turn my attention to today's observance of the Feast of the Holy Family.

What does it mean to be a holy family?

I assisted at a marriage ceremony yesterday. The Church teaches us that when a man and woman marry, they are called to lead their

37

new spouse to holiness. An extension of that obligation calls parents to lead their children to holiness. *All* families are called to be holy families.

That is a daunting task, especially when we are given Joseph, Mary, and Jesus as our example of what a holy family looks like. We can picture that first Christmas with the infant Jesus lying in the manger, and Mary and Joseph watching over Him. Kings bearing gifts, a bright star shining down, and a multitude of the heavenly host singing "Glory to God in the highest!" Now *that's* a holy family!

With apologies to my wife and children, I believe Joseph had a distinct advantage when it came to having a holy family; what a great start! My memory is not the greatest, but I am fairly certain there were no bright stars or kings when Carol delivered our children.

I know I did not hear a multitude of the heavenly host singing, but I do seem to recall Carol saying beautiful things to me during childbirth. Things like "Stop wiping my forehead, you're messing up my hair!"

It should be noted on this feast day that it was not the kings, the bright star, or the heavenly host that made Jesus, Mary, and Joseph a holy family.

It was Mary saying, "Yes," to what was being asked of her. It was her willingness to be the handmaid of the Lord. It was her complete faith and trust in God and accepting the responsibility to lead her family to holiness.

It was Joseph shaking off doubt and trusting in the words of the angel. It was doing everything in his power to protect his family and carry out God's will for them.

It was Jesus taking on human form in order to lead *all mankind* to holiness.

It was, for the entire family, acceptance, humility, and submission to God's will. In reference to this feast day, Pope Francis reminds and encourages families to "always live in faith and simplicity, like the Holy Family of Nazareth."

Faith and simplicity. When put it in those terms, the task seems a bit *less* daunting.

Mary was without sin, and Jesus was God incarnate. We could drive ourselves crazy trying to measure up to *the* Holy Family; but what we can do is give our best effort.

God knows we are not perfect. What He wants is for us to wake up each day committed to answering the call to personal holiness and the call to lead others to holiness as well. We should pray daily for His guidance in this effort, for His continued presence in our lives.

We will fail in our efforts at times. He knows that, and we know that. When we do, we seek forgiveness and do our best to get back on track, using "faith and simplicity" as our mantra.

If we are not continually moving forward in response to our call to personal holiness, there is no way we could be helping our family move forward in theirs.

⟨⟩

I have spent my time thus far focused on the nuclear family— mother, father, and children—but I believe the idea of holy family goes beyond that.

I believe we are being called to lead *all* our families to holiness:

- The men you bowl with, the ladies you play cards with, and the people you go out to dinner with—your family of friends
- The receptionist who answers your phones, the people you encounter while making sales calls, and the people you sit with in board meetings—your family of co-workers
- Your prayer group, fellow St. Pius parishioners, your high school community

The small groups and the large groups are *all* families.

We, the local Church and the universal Church, are called to lead one another to holiness. On this feast day, we look to the example of the holiest of families for inspiration. We acknowledge their unwavering acceptance, their humility, and their submission to God's will and endeavor to offer up the same.

We respond to Pope Francis' encouragement and do our best to "always live in faith and simplicity."

What does that look like?

To answer that question, we turn to today's second reading, St. Paul's Letter to the Colossians: "Put on heartfelt compassion, kindness, humility, gentleness, and patience. Forgive one another as the Lord has forgiven you. Put on love, and let the peace of Christ control your hearts. Be thankful."

That is faith and simplicity in action.

When we live in this way, we take steps toward leading everyone we encounter—our immediate family, our friends, our coworkers, and our Church—toward holiness.

We will be doing *our* part in creating and nurturing a holy family.

—December 2013

THROUGH THE EYES
OF YOUR HEART

Second Sunday of Ordinary Time 2014   *Isaiah 49:3, 5-6*
                                          1 Corinthians 1:1-3
                                          John 1:29-34

Two weeks ago, we celebrated the Feast of the Epiphany. The gospel told the story of the how the magi, guided by the star, came to a humble manger to bow down before the baby Jesus and bring Him gifts suitable for a king. We tend to think about the epiphany in terms of that one singular event.

It should be noted that acts of epiphany, of God revealing himself to His people, occur at other times in Scripture as well.

Last week was the Feast of the Baptism of Our Lord. After Jesus was baptized, the sky opened up and a dove came to rest on Him. A voice from the heavens said, "This is my beloved Son, with whom I am well pleased." God was once again revealing Himself to His people.

In today's gospel, as Jesus approached, John the Baptist announced, "Behold the Lamb, who takes away the sins of the world."

We will hear Father say those same words later in the Mass as he elevates the Eucharist. He will be revealing God to us.

The epiphany is not just a series of Bible stories. It is an ongoing phenomenon. If we are paying attention, God is continually revealing Himself to us.

To those who are *open*, there are "God moments" all around us.

⸺⫘⸺

Several years ago, my father-in-law was in hospice care in the hospital, and the family was being prepared for the fact that Joe was going to die.

My wife, Carol, her mom, and her sisters were spending most of their time at the hospital. They were all exhausted. I took some time off work to go and sit with Joe, hoping to give the girls a break and let them get away for a short time.

When I arrived, they went off to get something to eat, leaving Joe and I alone in his room. I sat in a chair along the wall, about three feet from Joe's bed. His system was shutting down, and we were told he was unaware of his surroundings. He was making agitated noises. There were random facial tics and jerking body movements. We were told the noises and movements were all involuntary.

I pulled my rosary from my pocket, leaned forward, and began to pray in an audible whisper. As I did so, Joe's agitation and movements seemed to lessen. I pulled my chair closer and continued praying the rosary, now slightly louder. Joe was again visibly calmer.

Finally, I pulled my chair right next to his bed and prayed the rosary aloud. For the next ten to fifteen minutes, as I prayed the rosary, Joe was completely at peace—no noises, no tics, no body movements.

There was no doubt in my mind that God was there in the room with us. It was a God moment, an epiphany.

⸺⫘⸺

I stood on a dirt road on a mountain overlooking the city of Port-au-Prince in Haiti. The devastation from the earthquake was unimaginable. Many thoughts ran through my head, including, *What am I doing? What good can I possibly do here?*

As I stood there in awe of the crumbled city, a little Haitian girl, maybe six years old, came alongside of me. She looked up at me as I looked down at her. She took my hand and stared at the devastation with me.

There was no doubt in my mind that God was holding my hand. It was a God moment, an epiphany.

<hr>

While these two examples are quite dramatic, God does not always reveal Himself in such dramatic ways. His presence is also made known to us in the simple events and interactions of our daily lives.

Our webmaster at school set up a website for the Christmas season that asked students to respond to the question "Where have you seen God in your life today?"

Here are just a few of the responses:

- I found God today in my younger siblings. They are always so happy and carefree. They love everyone and are so innocent.
- I found God with me today when I woke up in the morning and saw my parents. I began to think about how hard they work for me.
- I found God in my friends who lifted me up with positive words when I was having a bad day.

If you are a younger sibling or a parent or a friend, you should know that you have the power to reveal God to others. God's revelation can be very dramatic, but He also reveals Himself simply, most often through our interactions with others.

You may be asking yourself, "Why doesn't this ever happen to me?" We need to train our eyes to see God revealing Himself to us.

In his Letter to the Ephesians, Paul refers to seeing life *through the eyes of your heart.* He wrote, "May the eyes of your heart be enlightened, that you may know hope."

If we accept the fact that God reveals Himself to us each day, how do we train our eyes to see Him? How do we see through the eyes of our heart?

Like anything else, it takes practice. We have to be deliberate in our attempts and open to His presence. We need to focus our attention outward and allow God to work through others to touch our lives. We need to be thoughtful and reflective.

When you see life through the eyes of your heart, you may also discover that God is using *you* to reveal Himself to others.

—January 2014

ALLOW GOD TO LOVE YOU

Solemnity of Mary, Mother of God   *Numbers 6:22-27*
                                             Galatians 4:4-7
                                             Luke 2:16-21

The Catholic Church honors Mary multiple times throughout the year. We do so again today with the Solemnity of Mary, the Mother of God.

Catholics are often accused of being "Mary worshippers," elevating her to what appears to some to be divine status; but that is not what the Church teaches us about Mary. The *Catechism of the Catholic Church* says, "By her complete adherence to the Father's will, to his Son's redemptive work, and to every prompting of the Holy Spirit, the Virgin Mary is the Church's model of faith and charity" (CCC 967).

We don't worship Mary; we celebrate and aspire to her total submission to God's will, her humble yes to becoming the Mother of God.

While her yes is extraordinary in and of itself, there are two specifics of that yes that elevate it even more. First, the timing of the yes. It is widely accepted by scholars that Mary was thirteen or fourteen years old when God sent the angel Gabriel to her. Apparently, back in young Mary's time, drama had not yet been invented.

I have witnessed firsthand the dramatic world of teenage girls. Anyone who has ever been around young girls of that age knows that it is not the most agreeable or most unselfish time in their lives. The life of a thirteen-year-old girl is rarely focused on anything that does not revolve directly around *her*. With that comes resistance to *any* suggestions from the outside world, including angels. Having helped raise two daughters myself, I can attest to that.

A second feature of Mary's yes is its immediacy. She did not ask for some time to "sleep on it" or tell Gabriel that she'd get back to him. She did not ask lots of questions or demand qualifiers. Her response was simply, "I am the handmaid of the Lord. Be it done unto me according to your word."

As the Church tells us, Mary was the model of faith and charity. She was a model of faith because she believed and accepted, even without fully understanding. After all, that's what faith is. Perhaps what allowed her to do that was the same thing that allowed her to believe what the shepherds had to say in today's gospel. She could not possibly have understood all that was being said about her newborn baby. Rather than reject what was being said, Luke wrote that "Mary kept all these things, reflecting on them in her heart."

She was a model of charity because she sacrificed everything—specifically, control of her life— for the common good.

It is fitting that we honor Mary on January 1 each year as we consider our New Year's resolutions. My personal resolution for 2015 is the same one I have had the last several years: turn over control of my life to God.

The fact that my resolution is the same again this year tells me I have a long way to go. It is an ongoing battle. I want to be able to say, "Be it done unto me according to Your word." I want to be His handmaid, His servant, completely and without reservation; but I struggle to give up control.

What am I afraid of? Am I afraid that God won't get it right? If so, that's pretty arrogant.

No, I am afraid because it leaves me vulnerable. How can I prepare for what's coming if I don't know what He has in mind for me? I lack trust. A thirteen-year-old girl can completely submit to God's will, yet I am a coward.

Last weekend, I read the homily delivered by Pope Francis at Midnight Mass on Christmas Eve. I discovered that perhaps I am approaching my New Year's resolution from the wrong perspective. Rather than thinking of it in terms of giving up control, perhaps I should look at it as allowing God to love me.

I should replace something I want but don't need—control—with something I desperately want and need—God's love.

> *How do I welcome the tenderness of God? Do I allow myself to be taken up by God, to be embraced by him, or do I prevent him from drawing close? "But I am searching for the Lord"—we could respond. Nevertheless, what is most important is not seeking him, but rather allowing him to find me and caress me with tenderness. The question is: Do I allow God to love me? (Pope Francis)*

My revised New Year's resolution for 2015: I will allow God to love me.

Rather than reject His will because I do not understand it, I need to learn from Mary's example and reflect on it in my heart. I need to allow what Nehemiah described in today's first reading. I need to allow the Lord to let his face shine upon me and be gracious to me, for Him to look upon me kindly and give me peace.

Total submission to God's will, turning control over to Him, is simply a matter of allowing Him to love us—a valuable lesson modeled by a drama-free thirteen-year-old girl.

—January 2015

JOY, PRAISE, AND HONOR

The Epiphany of the Lord 2015　　　　　*Isaiah 60:1-6*
　　　　　　　　　　　　　　　　　　　Ephesians 3:2-6
　　　　　　　　　　　　　　　　　　　Matthew 2:1-12

Carol and I received a text from our daughter, Laura, on Christmas morning. It included a video intended to capture the reaction of our twenty-month-old granddaughter, Ellie, when she saw all the presents under their tree.

As Ellie ran toward the tree with excitement, all you could hear her say was, "Bow ... bow ... bow!" She went to each package and removed its stick-on bow. Once she had them all, she sat down and played with them, sticking them on her pajamas and in her hair.

Laura's text said, "We could have saved a lot of money. It looks like the perfect gift for Ellie would have been a pair of Elmo socks and a bag full of bows."

We admire those people who are able to give the perfect gift—not perfect because of how big it is or how much it cost, but because it says to the recipient, "I know you."

Those who receive the perfect gift are often caught off-guard. They didn't even realize that they wanted it or needed it. It wasn't on their gift radar. When they open it, you can tell by the expression on their faces—it is the perfect gift.

The people watching the opening of the gifts look at one another and nod, secretly wishing they had thought of it.

—⁂—

My daughter Mary started taking piano lessons when she was eight years old. I remember driving to her lesson one afternoon when Billy Joel's song "Piano Man" came on the radio. I was a big Billy Joel fan, so I turned up the radio and said to Mary, "Keep practicing and someday you'll be able to play like this."

She smiled and giggled. Five years later, on Father's Day, Mary handed me a gift. It was a cassette tape. I put it in the tape player, and "Piano Man" could be heard. But it was Mary playing the piano, knocking my favorite song out of the park.

On a Father's Day card, she wrote, "You said someday – today is the day!" It was the perfect gift—Mary knew me.

—⁂—

Carol has run a total of ten marathons at different cities around the country. The kids and I tried to go and support her at as many of them as we could. We went to her first two races but were unable to attend her third one, being held in Chicago. She understood, but it saddened her that we were not going to be able to be there to cheer her on.

When Carol checked into her room at the hotel, there was a small gift on her bed, with a note from Laura: "Don't open until after the marathon."

When she returned to the hotel after completing the race, Carol opened the gift to find a small tape player with a note, "Press here." When she pressed the button, there was a recording of the kids cheering for their Mom, shouting out how awesome she was, how much they loved her, and how proud they were of her.

It was the perfect gift—my daughter knew her mom.

<hr/>

Back in the early nineties, I was pretty sick. I was hospitalized here in Indianapolis for a week, then sent to a special hospital in Chicago where I needed to spend another ten days. Carol wanted to be near me, so she stayed in a hotel across the street from the hospital.

She was panicked. This was not something we shared with many people, but we did not have extra money. She knew staying there was going to completely wipe us out—mortgage payment, grocery money, and more would all be gone.

At the end of the week, when Carol went to check out, she was told that someone had paid the bill in full. We never did find out who did that for us.

It was the perfect gift—someone knew us.

<hr/>

The magi, presented to us in Matthew's gospel today, brought gifts for the newborn baby—the famous gifts we hear about each year on the Feast of the Epiphany. Gold was a symbol of royalty and divinity. They knew Jesus was going to be both God and King.

Frankincense was highly fragrant when burned and was therefore used in worship. It symbolized a priestly role. They knew Jesus was going to be both holy and righteous.

Myrrh was a spice used in anointing and embalming. It symbolized suffering and death. They knew Jesus was going to be the sacrificial Lamb.

While these gifts certainly show that the magi knew about Jesus, they were not the perfect gifts of the magi. The perfect gifts in the story receive little notice: In today's readings, we hear that the wise men were overjoyed. They proclaimed the praises of the Lord, and they prostrated themselves and did him homage.

The perfect gifts that day were not gold, frankincense, and myrrh. The perfect gifts were joy, praise, and honor. The magi not only knew *about* Jesus, they knew Jesus.

The Feast of the Epiphany celebrates God revealing Himself to us. The star above the manger, the words of the shepherds, and the appearance of the magi are all offered as evidence that Jesus is the Christ.

Next week we will celebrate the Feast of the Baptism of Our Lord. After Jesus was baptized, the sky opened up, and a dove came to rest upon Him. A voice from the heavens said, "This is my beloved Son, with whom I am well pleased." Revealed once again.

Multiple times throughout Scripture, God reveals Himself to us. He allows us to know Him. It is His perfect gift to us, and it is a gift that keeps on giving.

He is "unwrapped" for us each time we come to Mass and hear the words of consecration. During the Eucharistic prayer, Father will put his hands over the bread and wine; this action is called the epiclesis. You'll see me kneel at that time. Then Father will say these words, "Make holy, therefore, these gifts, we pray, by sending down your Spirit upon them like the dewfall." And then he will make the sign of the cross over the gifts and say, "So that they may become for us the Body and Blood of our Lord Jesus Christ."

Epiphany once again—God reveals Himself to us. Our humble offering of bread and wine become the perfect gift of the Eucharist right before our very eyes. It is just what we need, even if it was not on our gift radar. He knows us better than we know ourselves.

We are capable of giving God the perfect gift in return. We can love Him and love others. We can offer Him the gifts of the magi—not the gold, frankincense, and myrrh, but the joy, praise, and honor.

In doing so, we give evidence that we truly know Him.

—January 2015

WE ARE NOT THE HIRED HELP

Second Sunday of   1 *Samuel 3:3-10, 19*
Ordinary Time 2015   1 *Corinthians 6:13-15, 17-20*
                           John 1:35-42

In today's first reading, Samuel is called to be one of God's prophets.
He was confused about where the call was coming from. It took God
four attempts, but eventually Samuel was on board.

It's not the only time God has had trouble when calling prophets.
He appeared in a burning bush to call Moses, who had excuse after
excuse about why he shouldn't be the leader God wanted him to be.

And Jonah—God had to chase him all over, including into and out
of the belly of a whale, to get him to sign on as a prophet.

Which raises the question: Why does God make more work for
Himself?

I mean, He's God. Why put up with all of this nonsense? He could
have snapped His fingers and Samuel would have been a prophet. He
could have skipped the burning bush, tapped Moses on the shoulder,
and ordered him to go free the Israelites.

If He really wanted Jonah to be a prophet, why didn't He just make
it happen? Jonah 2:11 says, "The Lord then commanded the fish to
vomit Jonah upon dry land." Did God really need all of that drama,

not to mention all the mess? Why chase Jonah? Why didn't He just choose someone else?

The same question could be asked of Jesus regarding His efforts while on earth. Why did He make more work for Himself?

In today's gospel, John the Baptist saw Jesus coming toward him and said, "Behold the Lamb of God." Andrew overheard this and started following Jesus.

Really? This is how Jesus chose one of His apostles? Some random guy following him down the street? Wouldn't it have been much easier to handpick the best and the brightest to be His apostles?

The rabbis leading the religious communities at that time were surrounded by scholarly disciples. These disciples studied and trained for years before being sent out as learned leaders. Only the best were called. Only the best survived. They were unrelenting, faith-filled, righteous warriors.

Why didn't Jesus tap some of *those* guys on the shoulder, tell them He was God, and give them their marching orders? Instead, He made more work for Himself by calling common laborers: fisherman and farmers, even a tax collector. He trained them using parables, which they often had difficulty even understanding. They were men whose faith surged and faded. Doubt was always looming. Not warriors at all, but cowards who ran off at the first sign of trouble.

If God's ultimate goal was spreading the gospel message, His methods were inefficient at best.

However, God is not about efficiency. If He were, He would not have given man free will. God wants us to live the gospel message, not recite it. He's okay with messy.

He wants us to feel and experience. He wants us to love and needs us to suffer. He wants us to be challenged and grow stronger because of those challenges. He wants faith to be part of who we are.

God wants us to take ownership. When it's ours, we'll fight for it. We'll hold on to it.

—◉—

As parents, Carol and I had a unique distinction. According to our kids, we were the only parents *in the entire world* who did not give their children an allowance. As you can imagine, we were quite proud of that. To be recognized on such a global scale was humbling.

We would be presented with facts such as the following: So-and-so's dad pays him $10 every time he cuts the grass or shovels the driveway. Those parents give their kids $5 a week, and all they need to do is make their beds and take out the trash. And if they cleaned their room, they got extra. Raking leaves, vacuuming, washing dishes—each chore had a pay incentive assigned.

Given the fact that all the other parents in the world were putting out cash for this type of work, our kids challenged us on why we didn't do the same. Our answer: "We don't pay you to help with work around the house because it comes with being part of a family."

If they had asked for further explanation, I would have added this: "When you work at something, you become invested in it. The work has intrinsic value. It promotes teamwork, work ethic, and service for the common good. It shows appreciation for all we have. These are values that you will take with you into the world. We earn our keep. It's what families do. You're not the hired help."

I could have paid them, or anyone, to do the work around the house. But if I had, my kids would have had no sweat equity in the family, no sense of ownership.

—◉—

Back to the original question: Why does God make more work for Himself? He wanted Samuel and Moses and Jonah to have some skin in the game. He needed them to be invested, so He made them work for it.

When they were serving as God's prophets, they did it with passion because they had paid their dues. God's work became part of who they were; it defined them.

As for the apostles, what if Jesus *had* chosen the best and the brightest? Would they have lived the gospel with as much invested passion as those Jesus ultimately chose? The apostles were a ragtag bunch of laborers, sinners every one, but they were in the trenches with Jesus. They earned sweat equity. They experienced raw life.

The apostles were definitely not the most efficient group ever, but they were incredibly effective models of the faith. In fact, each of the twelve died for his faith. That's ownership.

What about us? What about this ragtag bunch of laborers?

"The harvest is plentiful, but the laborers are few." We are called to get to work.

Because God is God, He could have easily created us and placed us directly into heaven. Easier on Him, easier on us. Instead, He is investing in us, hoping we will invest in Him. We are on earth to earn sweat equity. We live life here so we can take ownership of our faith and show a commitment to living the gospel. Every bit of joy, sorrow, pain, suffering, and love we experience along the way is an investment in our faith. We earn our keep. It is what a family of faith does.

We are not the hired help.

—January 2015

INVITING JESUS TO THE PARTY

Second Sunday of
Ordinary Time 2016

Isaiah 62:1-5
1 Corinthians 12:4-11
John 2:1-11

While studying scripture during my deacon formation, three important things were emphasized.

First, scripture is the divinely inspired word of God. The scribes and evangelists were inspired to write down the message that God wanted us to hear.

Second, the messages found in scripture are timeless. Despite the fact that the words were written 1,500 to 2,000 years ago, the message still resonates today. That message may be buried in stories that are foreign to us—the sacrificing of animals, wandering in the desert, or fighting against the Philistines—but it is there nonetheless, and pertinent to our lives.

Finally, scripture is personal. When I read a scripture passage, I might get one message. Someone else may read the same scripture passage and get a completely different message. That does not mean one of us is right and one of us is wrong. We simply received the message *we* needed to hear on *that* day.

How many times have you listened to the readings at Mass and said, "That is just what I needed to hear today."

That's the Holy Spirit at work.

God speaks to us through scripture. That is why John begins his gospel by telling us, "In the beginning was the Word, and the Word was with God, and the Word was God."

There have been times when I have needed to prepare a homily for readings I have already preached about in the past. I spend time with the readings, and before I start writing, I read over my earlier homily. I am surprised that the message I got back then and the one I am getting now are different.

It makes sense since I am different. We change over time—the pace of our lives, our hopes and dreams, our wants and needs. Our faith can ebb and flow. Scripture is still rich and powerful, but its message evolves as I evolve. What God has to say to us evolves.

That is a long explanation, but the personal nature of scripture is fascinating to me and important for all of us to keep in mind.

Today's gospel is a good example. When I preached about the wedding feast at Cana in the past, my sole focus was on Jesus. I spoke about this day being the "coming-out party" for Jesus. It was the site of His first miracle and so "revealed his glory." It propelled His recently begun public ministry.

However, as I read and reread the gospel this time, two messages came through loud and clear, and neither was focused on the miracle itself or the public ministry of Jesus.

First, I found it interesting that John's account began with the words, "There was a wedding at Cana in Galilee, *and the mother of Jesus was there.*"

This alerts us to the fact that Mary would play a critical role in the story. Without Mary, there would have been no miracle that day. Without Mary, the ministry of Jesus would have been delayed. Her role was to prompt Jesus to begin His work, despite His objections, "My hour has not yet come."

Even more powerful is the recognition that in pushing Jesus forward in His public ministry, she was at the same time letting Him go. Letting Him go despite knowing what that would mean for her son. She demonstrated incredible courage and selflessness.

Second, and this is what I will concentrate on this morning, John's retelling of the story of the wedding feast at Cana offers us a beautiful template for how we should approach prayer and our relationship with Christ.

John tells us that Jesus was *invited* to the wedding. The first step in building a relationship with Christ is a willingness to receive Him into our lives, into our hearts. While He is ever present and willing to come to us, He will not force Himself on us. We must invite Him in. This takes courage. It takes trust. If we can establish that trust, or even if we can allow Him into our lives while staying guarded and doubtful, we open the door to His graces.

The gospel then tells us that a problem arose—they were out of wine. What are *you* "out of"? Are you an empty vessel? What causes that feeling of emptiness, and where do you turn? We must acknowledge our need and turn to Jesus. We saw that take place at Cana.

We also saw the power of intercession. The bridegroom was out of wine, so Mary interceded with Jesus on his behalf. Catholics are often questioned about our fascination with Mary. People want to know why we ask her to intercede for us.

Today you have your answer: "Because at the wedding feast in Cana there was no wine. Mary talked to Jesus … and suddenly, there *was* wine. Problem solved. We pray to Mary because Mary gets results."

So we bring our needs to Jesus, directly or perhaps asking for the intercession of Mary or the saints. We pray.

However, prayer is not a monologue. We must allow time to listen.

We get that message from today's gospel. Mary directed the servants, "Do whatever he tells you." We can't do whatever Jesus tells us if we don't take the time to listen.

Jesus will respond. He will respond to our needs. No longer empty, but filled to the brim. Filled not with water, but with wine. Filled not with the ordinary, but with the extraordinary.

John ends by telling us that in performing the miracle of turning water into wine, Jesus "revealed his glory, and his disciples began to believe in him."

As Jesus answers our prayers, our faith deepens. Like the disciples, our reliance upon Him and trust in Him grow.

The cycle of prayer is shared in the story of the wedding feast at Cana:

- We invite Jesus into our hearts.
- We share with Him our struggles and our needs.
- We ask Him for help.
- We listen and do as He guides our hearts to do.

Jesus responds, and in so doing, our relationship with Him is strengthened.

The wedding feast at Cana is not about running out of wine, and it is more than a simple retelling of a miracle story. It is a guide to prayer and to building a relationship with Jesus.

It is a reminder that the empty vessels would never have been filled if Jesus had not been invited to the party.

—January 2016

LENT

FILTERING OUT THE
NOISE IN YOUR LIFE

Second Sunday of Lent 2013   *Genesis 15:5-12, 17-18*
                                   Philippians 3:17-4:1
                                   Luke 9:28-36

When I was the director of Our Lady of Fatima Retreat House, we sponsored a program called Morning for Moms. We offered a morning retreat for the ladies in the upstairs conference room and provided babysitting services downstairs. There would normally be twenty-five to thirty little kids, from infants to preschool.

On one particular occasion, we were short-handed, and I was called upon to help with the babysitting. One of the babies, Patrick, who was sitting in a swing, began to cry. A staff member, Cheryl, started toward the swing to pick Patrick up and said to me, "Watch this, it's amazing."

By the time she had gotten to Patrick and taken him out of the swing, Patrick's mom was walking through the door.

Cheryl told me it happened all the time. There was a presentation going on in the conference room, the air handler was running full speed, the babies were on an entirely different floor of the building, behind closed doors—and yet, Patrick's mom heard him cry.

About twelve years ago, we invited a gentleman to our school to give a basketball free throw shooting demonstration. With seven hundred students sitting all around him on the gym floor, he proceeded to shoot one hundred free throws.

He was talking the whole time, kids were making noise, occasionally someone would walk across the lane in front of him, but nothing phased him.

He hit his first forty-one free throws and ended up making ninety-four out of one hundred shots.

Such demonstrations of focus amaze us, don't they? We marvel at someone's ability to block out all distractions and focus on whatever it is that is important to them—the cry of their child or sinking a free throw.

We are amazed when we see this, yet I'm sure we have all shown this same ability at one time or another. I know the girls in my family can attest to my ability to shut them out when there is a Colt's game on TV.

The ability to filter distractions is not a special gift; it comes out of desire.

For those of you who are in education, we see in today's gospel that God is an accomplished teacher. He implemented some very effective teaching methodologies.

Step 1: Grab the students' attention. When Jesus' *clothing became dazzling white*, Peter, James, and John became fully awake. He got their attention.

Next, the lesson: Moses is there, representing the law of the Church. There is Elijah, representing the prophets, those who had foretold of things to come. And with them is Jesus, whose divinity has been revealed to them, but who is also fully human and fully present to them. He was the "here and now."

Obviously, the disciples didn't understand the point of the lesson, so God summarized it for them: The law was important, and the words of the prophets were important—but if there was ever any conflict between the law and the prophets and the message of Jesus, you are to follow Jesus.

God could not have been any clearer in his parting words to Peter, James, and John up on that mountain: "This is my chosen Son. Listen to him."

—◦◦◦—

The Transfiguration is one of the Luminous Mysteries of the rosary. To be luminous means to radiate light, to radiate truth.

The disciples learned a valuable lesson directly from the source that day. But why was this necessary? Why the sense of urgency?

Jesus was preparing to head to Jerusalem. He knew that the disciples were still having difficulty understanding Him and His mission. Jesus was "taking it up a notch" with the disciples.

They had distractions all around: The scribes and Pharisees were criticizing many things Jesus and his disciples were doing. There were questions swirling around Jesus. Who was this? John the Baptist come back to life? A new, greater prophet?

And then there was their relationship with Jesus, this unusual man who was spreading a simple message of love for God and one another and encouraging them to do the same.

What, and who, were they to believe?

To help them focus on what was important, God radiated the truth through the Transfiguration and made absolutely clear his message: "This is my chosen Son. Listen to him."

It makes sense that the story of the Transfiguration is read during Lent.

During Lent, we too are called to take it up a notch, called to focus on that same message the disciples heard on the mountain: "Listen to him." Not to all the false voices of the world, but to Him.

This is easier said than done. Like the disciples, we have many distractions. A 2011 study on how Americans spend their time on average each day speaks to these distractions:

- Forty-one to seventy minutes each day is spent on personal grooming.
- Ninety minutes is devoted to household activities.
- Leisure activities, which would include running, going to the gym, watching television, surfing the Internet, visiting with friends, and other such activities, consume nearly four hours of our time each day.
- As for religious activities, including personal prayer, we spend on average just fifteen minutes.

There are many things that society, or our own selfishness, tells us are more important than our faith life. We need to be successful. We need to make money. We need to be beautiful. We need *things*. We need to be entertained. We need immediate gratification.

It is clear these things are distractions because they consume so much of our time.

Do we try to "squeeze in" five minutes for morning prayer but have no problem spending over an hour shopping online?

Do we say we would do more charitable work if we had the time and meanwhile spend three hours on the golf course or five hours a week in the gym?

Do we go to Mass and check it off the list, our commitment done for the week?

Do we neglect our obligation to take the gospel message out to the world?

What are *your* distractions? Are you able to filter these distractions and focus on what's important, like Patrick's mother and the free-throw shooter?

When God says to you, "This is my chosen Son; listen to him," do you hear him or does it just get lost in all the noise of your life?

—February 2013

FORTY-DAY DATE WITH GOD

Ash Wednesday 2014   *Joel 2:12-18*
                                        2 Corinthians 5:20-6:2
                                        Matthew 6:1-6, 16-18

Is it me, or is Lent kind of depressing?

It can be torture. We focus on fasting and sacrifice. There is no meat allowed on Fridays, so we will have to put up with a million commercials about fish sandwiches. We have to "give up" something we love: TV or pizza or soft drinks or video games. We hear scripture readings about people tearing their garments and crying out to the Lord in anguish. They sit in the dirt, beat their chests, and declare that they are unworthy.

In a few minutes, we will put ashes on your foreheads, because *you* are unworthy. You are nothing but dust. You'll fast, and you will like it or else.

And you need to go to confession. Why? Because you are all just a bunch of sinners, that's why.

We get to do all of this great stuff for *forty days*. Welcome to Lent!

That's one way of looking at Lent. Here's another: Lent invites us to look for ways to grow closer to God.

You say, "Well, we should be growing closer to God all year, not just during Lent."

That is absolutely true. Unfortunately, that is not part of our human nature. We get busy with things. We get caught up in the stuff of life. We spend less and less time focused on our relationship with God and more and more time focused on ourselves. We intend to spend time with God, but it just doesn't happen. If we have ten things on our to-do list, and we only have time for nine, most often it is time with God that gets cut from the list.

Lent is a time to refocus our lives and grow closer to God.

First question: *Why do we emphasize fasting and giving up things during Lent?*

Answer: These actions are sacrificial. We are saying, "It is not all about me." We acknowledge the sacrifice Christ made by making a sacrifice in return. I'm not sure giving up TV and not eating meat on Fridays compares to Jesus being nailed to a cross, but they are sacrificial gestures, and they direct our focus outward, away from ourselves. Sacrifice humbles us. The ashes we receive today humble us. After all, no one looks better with ashes on his head. With humility we acknowledge our sinfulness and wear the symbol of Christ's sacrifice, a cross, on our foreheads.

Our focus is on Him. As with any worthwhile relationship, we are putting the other person, or in this case, God, first.

Second question: *Why are we asked to spend more time in prayer and encouraged to go to confession during Lent?*

Answer: Can you imagine trying to grow a relationship with another person without ever having a worthwhile conversation? What kind of a relationship could possibly develop if the only time you spoke was a quick hello as you passed one another in the hallway? Or you only spoke briefly as you stood in the lunch line?

If we want to grow a relationship with someone, we need to spend time in conversation. We need to have open communication during which we feel comfortable sharing our ups and downs, our hopes, dreams, fears, and worries.

We need to be able to ask forgiveness when we make mistakes. That is what prayer and confession are all about—open, honest, loving communication with God. You build a relationship with God by having conversations with Him.

Third question: *Why are we encouraged to go to Mass more often and to spend time in Adoration during Lent?*

Answer: Because when we are developing a relationship, we want to spend time with that other person. Talking on the phone is great, and texting and messaging keep us in contact, but it is not the same as being in the same room with that person. It is not the same as face-to-face time.

The same is true of our relationship with God. Talking with God is awesome, but visiting Him is even better. He is truly present in the Mass. He is truly present at Adoration. He wants us to spend time with Him. Ask someone you love if they would rather get a phone call or a visit from you. What do you think they will say?

Final question: *Why do we emphasize almsgiving and service during Lent?*

Answer: These actions, like fasting, are sacrificial. However, there is more to it. Serving others and sharing our resources with them pays forward the gift of our relationship with God.

When you develop a relationship with a boyfriend or girlfriend over time, you want that person to meet your friends and your family. You want everyone to love and care for him or her as much as you do. You want to share the gift of your relationship with others. We express our gratitude and love for God by shouting it out to the world through our actions.

Finally, think about what causes most personal relationships to fail:

- The two people are no longer attentive to the needs of the other.
- The two people no longer share openly and honestly with one other.
- The two people spend less and less time together, so the relationship is not able to develop.
- The two people isolate themselves, failing to share the joy of their relationship with others. Eventually the relationship grows stagnant and dies.

Consider Lent a forty-day date with God. Be attentive to Him. Sacrifice your own needs in order to focus on Him. Talk with Him. Communicate openly and honestly. Share the real you. Visit Him regularly. Let Him know you want to see Him and spend time with Him. Share the joy of your relationship with God with others.

If we approach Lent in this way, it is possible that some of the habits we form will stay with us and continue to enhance our relationship with God long after Lent is over.

If we approach Lent as a depressing forty days of torture, we will likely break up with God as soon as Lent is over.

—March 2014

WHAT HAVE YOU DONE
FOR ME LATELY?

Third Sunday of Lent   *Exodus 17:3-7*
                              Romans 5:1-2, 5-8
                              John 4:5-42

When I am driving in the car, I often listen to sports talk radio. The day after the Colts or Pacers win, the callers are singing the praises of the coaches and players. The players are awesome! Best team we've had in years. The coach should be Coach of the Year.

The day after a loss, the coach doesn't know what he's doing. He's running the wrong offense. He's the worst coach we've ever had, and he should be fired. The day after a loss, the players stink, and they all need to be traded.

How quickly these sports fans forget. We live in a world that asks, "What have you done for me lately?"

It appears as though this same sense of entitlement was alive and well as far back as 1500 BC. In the first reading from the book of Exodus, we hear that the Israelites were thirsty. It reads, "The people grumbled against Moses, saying, Why did you ever make us leave Egypt?"

Make them leave Egypt? Really?

In the time leading up to this grumbling, God, working through Moses, had delivered the Israelites from over four hundred years of slavery, spared the lives of their firstborn sons, parted the Red Sea to allow them safe passage, destroyed the Egyptian soldiers who were pursuing them, made quail available for them to eat in the desert, and dropped manna from the sky.

Each time God saved them, the Israelites sang His praises.

How quickly they forgot these many blessings from God. Now, when they were thirsty, their praises quickly became, "But what have you done for me lately?"

Just like the fickle sports fan, they grumbled and said God should be traded or fired.

The mistake the Israelites made, and that we often still make today, was in thinking that God was only involved in the extremes of their lives. They only recognized His presence in the highest of highs and considered Him absent in the lowest of lows.

They praised Him for the highs and cursed Him for the lows.

They paid Him little attention otherwise. Why should they? After all, God is really only a factor in our time of need. When those times pop up, we call on Him for help. Sometimes He delivers and sometimes He doesn't.

Is that how we view our relationship with God?

He is only with us in the highs of our lives and abandons us in the lows? Where does He go in between? Where is He hiding?

What we often lose sight of is that God is *always* with us. There are countless moments in our lives when God reveals Himself to us and is truly present.

On the morning of the Israelites' grumbling, God had already revealed His presence in the form of many gifts: The fact that they woke up at all—God had given them the gift of another day. The gift of the earth upon which they walked. The gift of time with their family. God was present to the Israelites through these gifts.

We are given these same types of gifts daily. Unfortunately, these everyday gifts from God often get lost in the chaos and messiness of our lives. They are gifts that should be cherished but are all too often missed.

What exactly are we expecting when we think of God's presence in our lives? Seeing a burning bush? Experiencing a flash of light? Hearing a voice from the clouds?

These would all be really cool, but it is unlikely to happen that way for us.

God is much more likely to present Himself to us disguised as our spouse, our child, a friend, or even a passerby on the street. We are much more likely to experience Him in the breeze, in a whisper, or in the silence.

God is right there in the middle of all the chaos and messiness. He is present in the everyday events, in the simple, yet powerful *moments* he inspires. God is there when I watch my children hold their own children, and I am witness to the genuine love between them.

When I am fishing on a calm lake at five in the morning, God is there. When a student looks at me, smiles, and says "Good morning," God is there. Dinner with friends, praying with Carol, watching my granddaughter fall asleep in my arms, family game night, a long run, and in the silence that rarely comes—God is there.

And in sickness and death and financial struggles and relationship problems and when experiencing the pain of feeling that no one loves us—God is there too.

In the big blessings and the small blessings, in the challenges and the suffering, God is there.

God doesn't make happenstance appearances in our lives and then abandon us. He is in it for the long haul, every step of the way. Paul confirms this in his Letter to the Romans, saying, "The love of God has been poured out into our hearts."

What a beautiful image.

Maybe it was not a physical thirst that the Israelites were experiencing but a spiritual one. Perhaps they were afflicted with a thirsty heart. The Israelites were not open to experiencing God all around them. Their hearts were not open to the love God was pouring out and so had dried up and hardened over time.

Most of us won't have the opportunity to hear God speak directly to us like He did to Moses and the prophets or be able to walk side by side with Jesus and hear Him teach like His disciples. However, that does not mean He is not with us.

If our hearts are open, we will experience His presence in the gifts He gives us daily and in the sacramental moments He inspires. Then we will receive the love that God is pouring out into our hearts.

That is what He has done for us lately.

—March 2014

DESERT EXPERIENCE

First Sunday of Lent 2015
                                                           Genesis 9:8-15
1 Peter 3:18-22
Mark 1:12-15

After studying today's readings in the context of the Lenten season, two ideas emerged for me: the significance of the number *forty* and the concept of a *desert experience.*

Before I focused on something like desert experience, I wanted to get a sense of whether or not people had a common understanding of what a desert experience was and if they had perhaps endured one of their own. Via e-mail, I asked twenty-five people, a mix of high school students and adults, those very questions.

I received several great responses, but my favorite came from a young man who described a desert experience as the "exclamation point to a great meal." He went on to say that he had a desert experience on his last birthday, when he ordered the peanut butter chocolate cake at The Cheesecake Factory.

I didn't have the heart to tell him that what he was describing was a *dessert* experience.

The first reading from Genesis details the covenant established between God and Noah after the great flood. The flood was the result of "forty days and forty nights" of heavy rain pouring down on the earth.

In Mark's gospel, we heard the familiar story of the forty days Jesus spent in the desert, being tempted by Satan.

In addition to these two readings for today, the number forty is mentioned 130 other times in Scripture, including the story of Moses and the Israelites forty years in the desert, told in the forty chapters of the book of Exodus.

The number forty generally symbolizes a time of testing or trial. Noah and his family were being tested, taking a leap of faith to build the ark and then enduring forty days and nights of torrential rain.

It was a desert experience, without the desert.

They withstood the trial, maintained faith, and emerged from the ark able to enjoy a new relationship with God, a fresh start.

Jesus was tested in the desert for forty days. Strengthened by His own resolve and ministered to by angels, He withstood Satan's efforts to tempt Him. He emerged from the desert stronger and ready to begin His public ministry.

Moses and the Israelites endured forty years in the desert, emerging stronger and experiencing the joy of arriving at their new home.

In our own lives, many of us go through desert experiences, periods of trial and testing.

Here are some of the ways a desert experience was described by others:

- "a period of darkness"
- "on a journey, thirsting to be satisfied in some way"
- "a time when I find myself wandering aimlessly"
- "being all dried up inside, not being whole, being all alone"
- "a feeling of isolation"

- "feeling like you're the only one in the world struggling with whatever it is you are struggling with"

Summary: In the midst of a desert experience, we feel empty. Why does God abandon us when we are enduring a desert experience?

I would argue that the opposite is true. We abandon Him.

As is our human nature, when we need God the most, we turn to Him the least. When the going gets tough, we tend to go it alone. We wander in the desert instead of resting in God, trusting Him and letting Him guide us. This triggers a vicious cycle that makes us feel even more isolated and alone. It adds to our emptiness.

What sends us into the desert? Some personal examples that were shared with me include the following:

- A loveless marriage
- Mounting debt
- A rebellious child
- A terminal illness
- Addiction
- Mental illness and depression

Clearly not all desert experiences look the same, but they can feel the same. Here is what it felt like for a sixteen-year-old high school student:

> *I felt like I was being bombarded from all directions: school, friends, parents, church, and society in general. On top of everything else going on in my life, my mom was diagnosed with cancer and a blood clot in one of the chambers of her heart. It took a toll on me and on my beliefs.*
>
> *This is what led me to my desert experience last year. I "left" God for a while. I turned away from Him. It wasn't until I had an emotional encounter with a friend a few months later that I let God come back into my life.*

78

I allowed Him to fill me with faith and love. Doing this enabled me to see things differently, to see things in a more positive and understanding way.

I've come to accept that obstacles are going to come along that will test my faith, but I know now that I will overcome them.

Through my desert experience I learned that, with God, I am stronger than the influences around me. And I know He is with me now and always.

This young lady emerged from her desert experience stronger and more aware of God's presence.

A desert experience is humbling. What we discover is that while we may feel alone during our times of struggle, we are in fact never alone.

When teen suicides rocked several high schools earlier this year, many young people found themselves wandering in the desert, feeling alone and abandoned by God. They asked, as I'm sure many of us have asked ourselves at one time or another, "Where is God in this?"

Quite simply, He is wherever we need him to be. If we need to be angry at Him, He is there; we can let Him have it. If we need comfort, He will wrap His loving arms around us. If we just need to talk, no one is a better listener. If we simply need to sit in silence and reflect, we can be assured that He is sitting right beside us.

Involving God in our lives is what Lent is about. It is time set aside to reconcile ourselves with God, to humbly acknowledge that we cannot do it without Him.

We pray, fast, and give alms in an attempt to set things right with God. Lent is our forty days of testing and trial.

Whether we are in the midst of a desert experience or acknowledging that we have endured one in the past, Lent calls us to renew our relationship with God and seek forgiveness for the times we have abandoned Him.

If we do that, we will emerge from our forty days stronger and more aware of God's presence. We will be prepared to experience the joy of the Resurrection.

—February 2015

HELPING 3:16 GUY

Fourth Sunday of Lent   *2 Chronicles 36:14-16, 19-23*
                                     Ephesians 2:4-10
                                     John 3:14-21

Most of us have seen him many times. If you haven't seen him, just watch. He can be found with a painted face or a rainbow-colored wig in the end zone of nearly every college or professional football game. He is occasionally chased by security across a baseball diamond during a nationally televised game. He will pop up just about anywhere that people will see him or cameras will be present. He has even been on an episode of *The Simpsons.*

I am talking about 3:16 Guy. He is the one waving a sign with the words "John 3:16" written in marker or wearing a T-shirt with the same John 3:16 message.

Today's gospel includes this famous scripture passage. It is John 3:16, and it reads, *"God so loved the world that he gave his only-begotten Son, so that everyone who believes in him might not perish but might have eternal life."*

3:16 Guy has done his part by taking this message out into the world.

This message, presented in the midst of a fiercely competitive athletic contest, offers an interesting dichotomy. Sixty or seventy thousand people are packed into the stadium, cheering at the top of their lungs. There is nothing more important than winning that game.

Then the camera catches 3:16 Guy holding his sign, a subtle reminder to everyone that this game pales in comparison to what is, or what should be, most important in their lives—the knowledge that Jesus lived and died for us.

I spent quite a bit of time thinking about 3:16 Guy this past week. I think he fascinates me because he is so different from me. I cannot imagine ever painting my face or wearing a rainbow-colored wig for any reason and certainly not out in public or to a ballgame. A foam finger would be over-the-top for me.

Yet there he is, 3:16 Guy, painted face and rainbow wig, holding his sign and making sure the message gets out.

A couple of questions emerge: What is his motivation? Does he care that people point at him or that many make fun of him?

In the first reading, from 2 Chronicles, we heard, "Early and often did the Lord God send his messengers to them ... but they mocked the messengers of God ... and scoffed at his prophets."

We know about the prophets of the Old Testament. While a few enjoyed acceptance, many were rejected; some were even killed. Being a prophet was not easy work. Maybe that's why we don't see many prophets today.

Or do we? God anointed prophets for thousands of years to ensure that His message would be heard. Did He suddenly stop? Or are people such as 3:16 Guy modern-day prophets?

A prophet is a messenger of God, a person who speaks for Him. He or she witnesses to God and calls people to conversion. So the short answer is, "Yes, he is a modern-day prophet."

The longer answer is, "Yes, he is a modern-day prophet ... and so are we." 3:16 Guy is a prophet, and so are we.

At your baptism, you were marked with oil as a sign that you are consecrated to God and anointed by the Holy Spirit. Your anointing also was a sign that you are joined to Christ and share in his threefold mission as priest, prophet, and king.

It says in the *Catechism of the Catholic Church*, "Christ establishes the faithful as witnesses and provides them with the sense of the faith and the grace of the word. Lay people evangelize, that is, they proclaim Christ by word and testimony of life."

What does that mean? It means we are prophets, and we have work to do.

It doesn't mean that we will all be prophets in the same way. 3:16 Guy has his way, but his way won't work for me. There are other ways to do the work of a prophet as the *Catechism* directs us; that is, to "proclaim Christ by word and testimony of life."

How can we act as a prophet, proclaim Christ, "by word"?

- We do this when the words we speak lift up and affirm rather than ridicule or demean.
- We do this when we speak up for those who don't have a voice—the unborn, the homeless, the imprisoned, the poor, and the forgotten.
- We do this when we speak up to correct an injustice or defend the weak.
- We do this when we participate in the Mass, praying and singing in full voice.
- We do this when we share our faith with our children, not leaving their formation to chance.

How can we act as a prophet, proclaim Christ, "by testimony of life"?

- We do this when we serve others with a smile on our face.
- We do this when we are present to others and attentive to their needs.

- We do this when we attend the March for Life, gather in front of Planned Parenthood, take an active role in our parish, or involve ourselves in mission work at home or abroad.
- We do this when we take advantage of opportunities to grow our faith through retreats, adult education, or scripture study.

Any time we say or do something that lets people know that Christ is central to our lives, we are prophets.

"God so loved the world that he gave his only-begotten Son, so that everyone who believes in him might not perish but might have eternal life" (John 3:16).

An important message to share. Paint your face, put on your wig, and grab your sign. Proclaim Christ *by word and testimony of life*. Do whatever you need to do to get the work done, to fulfill *your* role as prophet.

I'm not sure I could ever be 3:16 Guy, but I like him. I think we need him, and I know he needs our help.

—March 2015

EASTER

POTTY TRAINING AND MORE

Third Sunday of Easter 2013

Acts 5:27-32, 40-41
Revelation 5:11-14
John 21:1-19

I am confident that Fr. Jim has never begun one of his homilies with this line: "Let's talk about potty training."

Our first child went through potty training by the book. She did everything just the way she was supposed to, and it was over and done with quickly and easily with no looking back.

It was a much longer, more difficult path with young Rick. He seemed to understand the concept of going to the bathroom on his own. He knew where the bathroom was. He liked his little step stool he got to stand on.

He had difficulty with two parts of the process: First, for whatever reason, he took off all his clothes to go to the bathroom. I don't know what else to say about that. That's just what he did. If we were good parents, we probably would have tried to break him of that habit, but it was just too funny to watch.

Second, he had trouble with timing. The time between the urge to go and actually going was pretty short. He was an energetic kid with lots to do, so he usually waited too long to head toward the bathroom, and when you add the time it took for him to take off all his clothes, he had many accidents. So it was a long, slow process.

He went from going to the bathroom in his pants, to going to the bathroom as he was getting undressed, to being naked and going to the bathroom in the hallway, then at the entrance to the bathroom, then on the bathroom floor, and so on. He kept getting closer, but he would be so excited about getting closer, that the excitement would cause him to go. The process took so long with Rick that Carol and I had a little problem maintaining enthusiasm. The happy potty dances and applauding and cheering him on began to wane.

But one day it happened. I was watching football on a Sunday afternoon, and Rick came running into the room, naked of course. "Daddy, I have to go to the bathroom!"

I said, "That's great, Ricky, you better get in there." And he took off to the bathroom.

Seconds later, he came running back out. "Daddy, I really have to go!"

"Okay, buddy, run to the bathroom!" And he did. Then I heard footsteps running back toward me. This time I was expecting him to tell me that he hadn't quite made it and let me know what area of the house I needed to clean up. But he came running back into the room, now hopping up and down with excitement.

"Daddy, I *really do* have to go potty!"

Just as I was about to encourage him once again to head to the bathroom, he grabbed my hand and said, "C'mon, I want you to *watch*!"

As if that wasn't cute enough, he added, "You're my best friend!"

That day, with his best friend cheering him on, he made it.

Cute kid story number two: When the kids were little, I made a big production out of coming home from work. I would make a lot of noise and take a long time working the key in the lock to build excitement. Carol would say to whichever kids were around, "I think I hear Daddy!"

So when I got in the door, somewhere between one and four kids would be lined up. I would kneel down, extend my arms wide, and yell, "Buddy!" And the kids would run or crawl toward me and jump into my arms. They would knock me over and roll around on the floor with me. Of course, because they were little kids, they would say, "Do it again, Daddy!" And we would have to repeat this dramatic entrance two or three more times.

―――

I shared these stories with you because I would like you to spend some time *thinking* like a child or remembering what it's like to *be* a child. Think about how as children we were so excited about life and saw each day as a new adventure. Think about how as children we were so accepting of others and so quick to forgive and forget. Think about how as children we were genuine and loving and pure.

I have heard this gospel reading many times over the years. When I read it in preparation for this weekend's homily, I noticed something I had never noticed before. I normally get caught up in the nets bulging with 153 large fish.

When Jesus appears on the shore, he calls out to the apostles, "*Children*, have you caught anything to eat?" That's odd. He called them *children*.

Then when Peter realized the man on the shore was Jesus, this grown man "jumped into the sea" and headed toward Him. Even though the boat was almost to shore and would arrive minutes later.

Jesus is home from work and is yelling, "Buddy!" And Peter is running to jump into his arms. For some, this may conjure up an odd
visual, perhaps even an uncomfortable image.

But it shouldn't. Many times Jesus spoke about our need to be like
children:

Matthew 18:3—"Truly I tell you, unless you change and become like
little children, you will never enter the kingdom of heaven."

Matthew 19:14—"Let the children alone, and do not hinder them
from coming to Me; for the kingdom of heaven belongs to such as
these."

Luke 18:17—"Whoever does not accept the kingdom of God like a
child will not enter it."

Jesus is telling us that we need to embrace our faith with childlike
exuberance, the same exuberance little children show in embracing
the people and the moments of their lives.

The resurrected Jesus stood on the shore and called out to the apostles, "Children, have you caught anything to eat?" By saying, "children," He is reminding each of the apostles about the need to become
like a little child. Peter, called to be the Rock of our Church and who
was believed to be the oldest of the apostles, sets the example with
his childlike response to Jesus' call by jumping into the water and
running to Him.

This gospel certainly speaks to what the Easter season is all about. We
view Lent as a penitential season. We put ashes on our foreheads to
signify our understood brokenness. We fast. We sacrifice. We emphasize the sacrament of Reconciliation.

But with Easter, we celebrate fifty days of joy and exuberance. Christ
died for our sins to bring us to new life and then rose from the dead
and is with us every day. Through Easter renewal of baptismal vows
we are reborn as children, His children. Jesus has his arms extended
and invites us to run to Him. He wants to be our best friend. He

wants us to jump up and down with excitement and take His hand. He wants to be invited to come with us and be a part of what we are doing. He wants to be invited to share in our lives, to comfort us in our sorrow, and to share in our joy.

He wants to be there to congratulate us on our accomplishments: whether that is running our first marathon, getting out of our comfort zone by serving the poor, or doing something as simple as going to the bathroom on our own for the first time.

—April 2013

BIRTH OF A NEW KIND OF FAITH

Fifth Sunday of Easter 2013

Acts 14:21-27
Revelation 21:1-5
John 13:31-33, 34-35

This past Tuesday at 1:30 a.m., Carol and I became grandparents for the second time. Our daughter Laura delivered a healthy baby girl, Ellie, the first child for her and her husband, Joey.

I told Carol I was going to announce it at the beginning of my homily. She said, "You can't do that!"

I said, "Watch me."

While this is a self-serving announcement, the announcement of a birth actually fits in quite well with today's readings.

On Sundays, the three readings are chosen based on a common theme. A thread runs through them and connects them. Today's message is of a fresh start, a clean slate, giving new birth; however you want to say it, the three readings all speak to a new beginning.

In the first reading from Acts of the Apostles, we hear the disciples "reported what God had done with them and how he had opened the door of faith to the Gentiles."

A new chapter is opened as the word of God is made available to the Gentiles. The Gentiles were considered a lesser people, perceived as uneducated and unsophisticated. They were certainly not on par with the Jews, yet the disciples brought the word of Jesus Christ to them, answering the call to "go out and make disciples of *all* men." It was a new beginning, a fresh start.

Today's second reading from the book of Revelation begins, "Then I, John, saw a new heaven and a new earth." The game had changed. The death and resurrection of Jesus Christ changed everything we thought we knew. The heaven and earth we had in our minds suddenly had a whole new look. It was the birth of a *new* heaven and earth.

Finally, from today's gospel, "I give you a new commandment: love one another." The law of Moses proved to be insufficient. Jesus offers us a new comprehensive yet simple law: love one another.

A new law, a new vision of heaven and earth, offered to all people, Jew and Gentile alike—the birth of a new kind of faith.

—⁂—

As a young boy, I loved to write stories. In third grade, one of the activities we did each week was called "free writing." The teacher would write the beginning of a sentence on the board, and for homework, we were to finish the sentence and use it to write a creative story. So there might be the beginning of a sentence that read, "Billy was so surprised when … ."

I would begin a story that said, "Billy was so surprised when he walked into school and realized that all the teachers had been taken over by aliens." My story detailed how my best friend and I fought the aliens and eventually saved the world. It ended with a parade in my honor and a medal from the mayor. But week after week, I received my papers back with red pen marks on them. The teacher wrote, "Your story is too long. Keep it to two pages" or "Your penmanship needs work" or "You should have a question mark here, not a period."

Eventually, my enthusiasm waned, and I simply went through the motions of fulfilling the assignment. I kept it to two pages. I took my time and printed neatly, careful to use correct punctuation. I fell in line and, as was expected, did the minimum.

In fourth grade, I had a new teacher, Mrs. Dunbar. She used the same weekly assignment as our third-grade teacher did, giving us the start of a sentence and asking us to finish the story.

I remember the first assignment. I went through the motions and did what was expected. A couple of days later, Mrs. Dunbar stood in front of the class and asked what was wrong with us. She said, "I almost fell asleep reading these stories! Where is your sense of adventure? Where is your creativity?"

Mrs. Dunbar opened up a door for me. She gave me a clean slate and asked me to create something special. She gave birth to a new way of doing things.

From that time on, I wrote story after story. Sometimes they were ten or fifteen pages long. The papers still came back with red marks on them, but Mrs. Dunbar wrote, "This is so exciting!" or "I want to hear more!"

She could sense my excitement, so she gave me extra writing assignments to do and would often ask me to read the stories to her.

Sorting through all of todays' readings, I thought of Mrs. Dunbar and how she had opened new doors. The assignment was the same. There was still structure, but she gave birth to a new way of doing things that brought joy and excitement.

The Acts of the Apostles: Mrs. Dunbar as one of the apostles, saying, "Sure, spreading the good news to the Jewish people is great. But wouldn't it be cool to take the message to the Gentiles too? Imagine what new and exciting things might be possible!"

The book of Revelation: Mrs. Dunbar as John, saying, "The way we used to view heaven and earth works okay, but what if we opened ourselves up to this new, exciting, inclusive view of heaven and earth? Imagine the world we could create!"

The Gospel of John: Mrs. Dunbar as Jesus, saying, "The commandments we have are worthy of our attention and we should not stray from them, but surely there is more. There is something missing. We need to bring new life to the laws we live by. *I give you a new commandment: love one another.*"

Easter Sunday did not end the Easter season, it started it. It started with a renewal of our baptismal promises. We have a rebirth of our commitment to the faith.

Our readings reflect this Easter message. How do we live out the messages we hear today? What does that look like in real life?

We reach out to the Gentiles when we lovingly invite someone back to the Church. How many fallen-away Catholics are just waiting for someone to invite them to come home? What would happen if we said, "Why don't I pick you up on Sunday morning, we'll go to church and then out to breakfast?"

We live out the message from the book of Revelation when we embrace the new heaven and earth of which John speaks. We embrace a new heaven and earth when we express our gratitude to God for all our blessings. This gratitude is expressed in words of prayer as well as by living a prayerful life and when we are good stewards of all He has given us. We embrace a new heaven and earth when we are a peaceful people. That peace comes from knowing that Jesus is present among us every moment of every day.

The message of today's gospel is pretty clear: love one another. We may think to ourselves, "This is an easy message to live out. I love lots of people." I am sure that is true. We love our family and friends. While Jesus' commandment does call us to love our family and friends, He challenges us to do much more than that. As simple as it sounds, "love one another" as Jesus means it can be very difficult.

Can we love someone who has hurt us? Hurt us not once, but over and over again? Can we love someone who has views and opinions that are the opposite of ours? Can we love the elderly, the homeless, and the poor? Can we get past our envy and love those who have more than we do or who we perceive to have "better" lives? Can we love someone who has rejected us? Someone who does *not* love us?

God loves us when we are deserving of His love. He loves us *the most* when we deserve it *the least*. This is what we are called to do as well.

When Jesus tells us, "Love one another," He means *everyone*. He means *always*.

When this happens, we will experience the new heaven and earth John saw revealed to him. We will give birth to a new, stronger faith.

—April 2013

Speaking in Tongues

Pentecost Sunday 2013　　　*Acts 2:1-11*
　　　　　　　　　　　　　　1 Corinthians 12:3-7, 12-13
　　　　　　　　　　　　　　John 20:19-23

Everyone knows the story of Pentecost. The apostles had locked themselves in a room, afraid to go out and face the world without Jesus. The Holy Spirit entered the room in the form of tongues of fire flickering over their heads. They were filled with the power of the Holy Spirit and suddenly found themselves with the courage to unlock their doors, step out, and begin preaching the gospel message.

The Holy Spirit gave them a voice.

The most amazing part of the gift they received was that all who heard them were able to understand. People from foreign lands, speaking many different languages and dialects, could understand what the apostles had to say. Each heard the apostles in his own language.

How is "speaking in tongues" even possible? Maybe it is not as mysterious as it sounds.

⸻

My wife, Carol, has been to El Salvador seven times. We have pictures of her in a small village, looking like the Pied Piper, surrounded by smiling Salvadoran children. Carol sketched out a mural on the side of the simple structure serving as the community center, and all the children were helping her paint it. Big smiles on their faces, paint everywhere.

Each time she goes there, she comes home with stories of what beautiful people the Salvadorans are. She comes back enriched by her relationship with them.

One year, I had the opportunity to go with her to El Salvador. When we arrived at the village, young people called out, "Carolina!" and ran to her, and gave her big hugs.

It was not until then that it dawned on me, *Carol doesn't speak Spanish!*

I watched her all week, stumbling over even the most basic Spanish words and phrases. But she smiled and she laughed and she touched them and hugged them. She cried with them and worked side by side with them. She let them know she cared about them.

She was speaking the universal language of love.

They understood her. She must have been speaking in tongues.

I learned from Carol. When I had the chance to go to Haiti, I tried to follow her lead.

The Haitians speak Creole. My French background could have helped me, but any French I learned in high school left my head the minute I walked out of the last class.

I was assisting on a medical mission. I held sick babies. I held elderly Haitians' hands as I took their temperature or their blood pressure. I smiled at them and lightly rubbed their backs. I had the opportunity to sit side by side with them in an earthquake-ravaged chapel and pray with them.

I spoke the universal language of Jesus, of love.

They understood me. I guess I spoke in tongues.

My son and daughter-in-law went on a trip to India with their church. In India, there are over 450 languages spoken.

Gendercide is rampant in India. Many female babies are aborted, killed in infancy, or abandoned. Rick and Whitney went to visit several all-female orphanages run by the Catholic Church. They played with the girls and hugged them. They laughed with them and loved them. And they sent the girls the powerful message that they have value.

They never spoke to the girls in their native language, but they spoke the universal language of the love of Jesus Christ.

The girls understood Rick and Whitney. Maybe they were speaking in tongues.

About three years ago, I was at a retreat led by Fr. Jim. Late one evening, he got a call from a family at the hospital.

Their sister was dying, the caller said. Could he come to the hospital and be with her?

It was snowing pretty heavily, so Father asked if I would drive him. When he arrived at the hospital and entered the visitors lounge, the family almost immediately became more calm. He talked with them for a few minutes, and they directed us to their sister's room.

It was just the sister, Fr. Jim, and I in the hospital room. Machines and tubes were everywhere, a respirator pushed out air.

In silence, Fr. Jim took the hand of the dying woman in his and began stroking it with the fingers of his other hand. Then he began to hum. A nurse walked in and stood still so as not to disturb anyone. Then he began to sing.

Before that night, I would never have described Fr. Jim's singing voice as beautiful. Loud maybe. Powerful, but probably not beautiful.

But when he began to sing "Amazing Grace," it was some of the most beautiful singing I had ever heard. The nurse was visibly moved. She heard the song as she needed to hear it. The woman who lay dying heard the song as she needed to hear it. I heard it as I needed to hear it. We each heard it in our own language.

He was using the universal language of love, even when he was saying nothing at all.

And when he sang, he must have been singing in tongues.

—

I could give another dozen examples of people I've seen communicating through the common language of love, and never once did I see a flame flickering over anyone's head. The power of the Holy Spirit was very much alive in each instance.

You speak in tongues each time a friend comes to you in pain. You may not be able to relate to her specific problem, but you offer support, encouragement, and consolation.

You do it each time you smile and greet a stranger.

You do it each time you step out of your comfort zone and serve others.

We hear the story of Pentecost not to remind us that the apostles were given an exclusive gift of the Holy Spirit but to let it be known that the gift of the Holy Spirit is available to all of us. It is available on demand and ready to be used.

The Holy Spirit gave the apostles a voice to be used to spread the gospel message.

I'm not sure exactly what happened on that Pentecost day. Did the apostles suddenly have the miraculous ability to speak in any language? Did those listening suddenly have the ability to understand what was being said, regardless of the language spoken? Or did the apostles step out from behind their locked door, joyfully singing the praises of Jesus Christ? Did they have smiles on their faces?

Maybe they hugged those who were suffering and in need of encouragement or comfort. Perhaps they extended a helping hand to the poor.

Maybe there was no mystery or miracle to it at all. Maybe the apostles simply spoke the language of the gospel message, the universal language of love.

Maybe the real gift the Holy Spirit gave the apostles that day was the courage to unlock their door.

—May 2013

FOREHEAD BONKS

Third Sunday of Easter

Acts 2:14, 22-33
1 Peter 1:17-21
Luke 24:13-35

In the early seventies, the makers of V-8 Juice began running TV ads that included the now-famous line, "I could've had a V-8!" The slogan has stood the test of time, and the company is running similar commercials even today. The premise of the ads was that after eating something *unhealthy*, the person in the commercial would suddenly realize that the better option would have been to have the healthier alternative, V-8 Juice. Upon making this discovery, they would smack their foreheads with the palm of their hand and say, "I could've had a V-8!"

Through a Google search, I learned that the palm-to-forehead smack in the commercials is referred to as a forehead bonk. The forehead bonk translates to "I wasn't thinking straight. I missed out on a great opportunity." The bonk is apparently intended to put the brain back in its proper place so the same mistake is not made in the future.

I found myself thinking of these V-8 commercials when I reread the familiar story of the Road to Emmaus in Luke's gospel today.

Jesus walked for miles with two of His disciples without them knowing it. How did this happen? They *knew* Jesus. As disciples, they had followed Him from place to place. They had sat for hours hearing Him preach and had grown to love Him. Yet the entire time He walked with them, they thought He was just another traveler on the road. Luke tells us, "Their eyes were prevented from recognizing him."

Later, these same disciples recognized Jesus in the breaking of the bread. Their eyes were opened. I can picture the disciples giving themselves forehead bonks and saying, "Jesus *is* alive!"

The central question to consider is this: What was it that prevented their eyes from recognizing Jesus? We are given no evidence to indicate that there was anything wrong with their eyes or that Jesus was wearing a disguise.

What kept those disciples from recognizing Jesus was *doubt*.

From their perspective, they had no *reason* to believe that the person who walked next to them was Jesus. After all, they had seen Him crucified with their own eyes. Jesus was dead and buried. He had hinted about rising from the dead. Scripture foretold of such things. They had even heard rumors that Jesus' tomb had been found empty. But people don't rise from the dead.

As much as they had hoped and prayed for the coming of the Christ, being eyewitnesses to His crucifixion and death made it difficult to believe that Jesus truly could *be* that Christ. Despite their own hopes, the promises made by Jesus, and the support of Scriptures, they still doubted. Their doubt prevented them from recognizing that Jesus was in their midst. Jesus was alive.

Like the disciples, doubt is often what keeps us from recognizing Jesus in our midst. We seem to be able to recognize Jesus in the good times. We trust because our productive, successful, happy lives are evidence that Jesus is alive.

Our trust is challenged in the tough times. A loved one is sick, and we may feel Jesus has abandoned us. We lose our job, and it is difficult to recognize Jesus in our lives. Relationships with spouses, children, or friends go through a rough patch, and we feel alone.

When we doubt Jesus, doubt that He is alive and active in our lives, our eyes are prevented from seeing Him. But He is traveling with us on our Road to Emmaus.

He is the nurse who is taking such good care of your loved one. He is the coworker who comforted you and encouraged you when you lost your job. When you are feeling alone, He is the one you are pushing away.

As disciples of Jesus who want to trust, who want to believe, we leave the door cracked open, hoping He is alive. At some point, we experience Him in the actions of others. We recognize Him in "breaking of the bread" type moments.

We may find ourselves bonking our own foreheads and saying, "Jesus *is* alive!"

We realize two things at that point: First, Jesus had been with us all along. Second, we missed out on something special during our time of doubt. We missed out on an opportunity to grow in our relationship with Jesus.

Today's readings describe what it is like to feel the presence of God, to know that Jesus is active in our lives *and* alive in our hearts. From today's first reading from Acts: "I saw the Lord ever before me … Therefore my heart has been glad."

In the gospel, the disciples on the Road to Emmaus, upon realizing that Jesus had been with them all along, say, "Were not our hearts burning within us?"

When doubt is removed, when we trust in His presence, our hearts too can experience the gladness; our hearts too can burn within us. I would much rather have a heart burning with the love of Jesus than to have the headache that comes from a forehead bonk.

—May 2014

WRING OUT THE SPONGE

Wednesday of the Third Week of Easter   ***Acts 8:1-8***
                                                 John 6:35-40

"I am the bread of life; whoever comes to me will never hunger" (John 6:35).

Think about the number of times bread is mentioned in scriptures. God dropped manna from heaven to feed the Israelites in the desert. Jesus multiplied the loaves and fishes in feeding the five thousand. At the Last Supper, Jesus offered the apostles bread, saying, "This is my body." The disciples on the Road to Emmaus recognized Jesus in the breaking of the bread.

Think about how important bread is. When you hear that a huge winter storm is on its way, what's the first thing to fly off the shelves?

Bread is a staple food for many. My wife has traveled many times to El Salvador. She tells me that the women of the village spend a majority of their day focused on bread—grinding the corn, kneading the dough, and baking it over the fire—making sure they have enough bread to feed their family. Bread is survival.

When I was young, I used to go to the Wonder Bread Bakery on the south side of Indianapolis with my mom.

I loved going. It was an opportunity to be with my mom one-on-one. With six kids in the family, getting individual attention was tough. Another reason I enjoyed it had to do with the bakery employees. They were so happy. They all had smiles. They gave me a paper baker's hat and sometimes let me into the back room where the baking was done and allowed to me push some of the buttons on the machines.

I remember asking my mom why everyone there was so happy.

She responded, "They're happy because they are making something everyone needs. How nice to be able to do that."

Later in the Mass, we will pray the Our Father together. We will say the words, "Give us this day our daily bread." When we pray these words, what are we really asking of God? Are we really asking for actual physical bread? Are we asking God to make us a sandwich every day? No, we are asking Him to feed us. To fill us spiritually. To give us what we need to sustain our faith.

We must guard against this becoming one-sided. We shouldn't be receivers only. We should not only be fed but feed others as well. It is the difference between having an active or a passive faith. It's not enough to sit back passively and say, "Okay, Lord, do your thing to me. Give me faith."

We need to be sponges. Yes, we need to soak in all that God has to offer us, but then we need to wring ourselves out and share it with others.

We need to radiate the faith!

Our faith comes through in how we treat one another, how we talk to one another, how we lift up and affirm one another, how we hold one another accountable, and how we love one another.

When we do all of these things, we are radiating our faith. We are feeding others. *We* become the bread of life, which is exactly what God had in mind.

—May 2014

THE HOLY SPIRIT IS
YOUR VOICE

Pentecost Sunday 2014   *Acts 2:1-11*
                           1 Corinthians 12:3-7, 12-13
                           John 20:19-23

Pentecost is our reminder that we're not alone.

Certainly the Christmas and Easter seasons are awesome, but for me, there is something special about Pentecost.

With Christmas, our Savior comes into the world: a gift of hope from the Father to us.

Through the passion, death, and resurrection of Jesus at Easter, we are the recipient of the ultimate sacrificial gift. A gift intended to save us from ourselves.

Christmas and Easter are gifts *for* us. Pentecost is a gift to be used *by* us. Through the gift of the Holy Spirit, we are given the courage to get to work.

In my theological studies, efforts to fully understand the concept of the Trinity nearly made my head explode. Three persons, one nature, Triune God. The one thing I did understand was why it was called a mystery.

One concept I heard that gave me a greater appreciation of the Trinity was this: The Father is our Creator, the Son is our Teacher, and the Holy Spirit is our Voice. Together they are God.

The power of the Holy Spirit led the apostles to set aside their fear and unlock their doors. The power of the Holy Spirit gave them a voice and the courage to use it.

The role *preparation* plays in our readiness to receive the Holy Spirit is often overlooked.

—⟨⟨⟨∩∪∩⟩⟩⟩—

As part of our formation as deacons, we spent an intensive week at St. Meinrad learning how to preach. The homiletics instructor shared the following story:

A young priest, Fr. Joe, watched his more experienced pastor step away from the ambo each time he gave a homily. He brought no papers with him, no note cards. He would walk in front of the congregation, take a moment to gather himself, and begin speaking. After watching this time after time, Fr. Joe finally asked the pastor how he was able to deliver a homily without having a script, or even any notes, with him.

The pastor responded, "It's the power of the Holy Spirit."

The young priest thought about how much time he spent writing homilies, struggling to put his thoughts into words, throwing away drafts, and starting over again. Maybe he should simply rely on the Holy Spirit. He decided to give it a try.

The week leading up to his weekend to preach, Fr. Joe did nothing to prepare. When he read the gospel, he was reading it for the first time.

Afterward, he walked away from the ambo to deliver a homily. He stepped in front of the congregation. He took a deep breath and gathered himself as he had seen his pastor do so many times. Then he waited for the Holy Spirit to give him the words he needed, to supply him with the homily that the congregation needed to hear.

And he waited. And waited.

Just as the young priest was beginning to panic, he felt a breeze and a soft whisper in his ear.

The voice said, "Joe, this is the Holy Spirit. Why aren't you saying anything?"

Fr. Joe realized he was on his own and stumbled through a miserable homily.

When he returned to his chair, the experienced pastor leaned over and said, "I guess I should have said the power of the Holy Spirit *and* hours of preparation."

The moral of the story, our instructor told us, was that the Holy Spirit helps those who are prepared to receive Him.

————

The apostles may have been afraid and appeared to lacked courage, but they were prepared when the Holy Spirit came upon them.

Advent is a time of preparation for Christmas. Lent is a time of preparation for Easter. The Easter season is a time of preparation for Pentecost, for the coming of the Holy Spirit.

If you have been following along, you may have noticed that we have been hearing readings from the Gospel of John the entire seven weeks of the Easter season. Most of these readings are part of what is called the Last Supper Discourses, or Farewell Discourses. They are Jesus' parting words to the apostles. He was instructing them, preparing them for what was to come. Preparing them for His death and for the certain persecution each of them would face because of Him. He prepared them by teaching them about love and sacrifice and about the joy of eternal life.

Jesus also assured them that they would not be alone. At one point, He said, "I will not leave you orphans. I will send you an Advocate."

He prepared them for the coming of the Holy Spirit.

I am sure that the apostles could not comprehend all that was being said since Jesus was still with them and they could not know all that was about to happen. But they listened and filed His words away for later. They were prepared when the time came.

Jesus did not say that He would send the Holy Spirit to do everything for them. He was not sending the Holy Spirit to do what the apostles were capable of doing on their own. He said they would not be alone, that He would send an Advocate—a supporter, a counselor, a cheerleader, an affirmer.

The Holy Spirit did not give the apostles the ability to live out the message of love, to preach to the people, or to baptize in the name of Jesus. Jesus had prepared them for over three years to do those things.

The Holy Spirit gave them the support they needed to get out of their chairs, offered affirmation, and eased their fear. The Holy Spirit unlocked the door for them. The apostles did the rest.

What does this mean for us? The Holy Spirit is fully available to all of us. The Advocate has been sent and is at our disposal.

The question is, are we prepared? Are we grounded in our faith? Are we open to the gift? Or does our fear and doubt blind us to the gift of the Holy Spirit and keep us locked up?

We are all sinners, but if we try our best to live the gospel message, if we take time for prayer, if we love and serve others, then we are prepared.

There will be times that you are struggling. You know the right thing to do or say because you are prepared, but you may be frozen with fear.

You are not alone. The Holy Spirit is available to you. Reach out and ask for help.

The gift has already been given and will be there at your side, supporting you, and cheering you on.

The doors keeping you from going out into the world will be unlocked.

The Holy Spirit is your voice.

—June 2014

Repentance and Conversion

Third Sunday of Easter 2015   *Acts 3:13-15, 17-19*
                                                  1 John 2:1-5
                                                  Luke 24:35-48

If you are a parent of more than one child, you may have experienced this. Two of your children get into an argument. One of the children ends the argument by pushing, kicking, punching, or saying something mean to the other.

You step in at that point. You bring them together, and you demand that the aggressor apologize to the offended.

The child rolls his eyes and mumbles, "I'm sorry."

Because he mumbled, you require him to try again. With full-blown attitude, he says, "I'mmmmm sooorrrrrry."

You are a persistent parent, and you know that's not good enough. So you look the child in the eye and you insist, "Say it like you mean it!"

———

I am fortunate that in our thirty-two years of marriage, Carol and I have never had a disagreement or done anything to hurt one another. (Just kidding, of course.)

So speaking hypothetically only, let's say that one of us *did* hurt the other. As long as we are being hypothetical, let's say it was me that hurt Carol.

Since I am a male, I would not sense on my own that I had hurt Carol, but her demeanor would make it clear that something was wrong. Through a process of elimination, I would discover that I must have done something or said something to hurt her. Connecting the dots, I would know that an apology was in order.

I would go to her, and in my most sincere voice, I would apologize for having hurt her. I might even add a hypothetical hug. Thinking my work was done, I would then turn to leave, only to hear from Carol: "*Saying* you're sorry isn't enough. You need to prove it by your actions."

—⫯⫯⫯⫯⫯⫯—

These memories came to mind as I reflected on the scripture readings for this third Sunday of Easter. In all three of today's readings, there is talk about sin and repentance. That surprised me.

I understand why we do that during Lent, but it's Easter! Didn't Jesus die for our sins?

We heard in the First Letter of St. John, "He is expiation for our sins, and not only for *our* sins but for the sins of the whole world." I had to look it up, but *expiation* means atonement.

Jesus paid our debt! The slate was wiped clean! These are words of celebration, so why are we being told to repent in today's readings?

In the gospel, Jesus quoted scripture saying, "Thus it is written that the Christ would suffer and rise from the dead on the third day and that repentance ... would be preached in his name to all the nations ... " This confirms that Jesus died for our sins.

However, forgiveness of sins is not the end of the story; it is only the beginning. Again, "*repentance* ... would be preached in his name."

During Lent, we are encouraged to go to confession, to seek forgiveness for our sins. The Lenten season ends with Jesus' sacrificial death on the cross. His death opened the door to salvation for all of us.

With the door open, we must act. We must step across the threshold. Christ's sacrifice was all for naught if we don't take that next step. That next step is repentance, stepping away from sin and toward what is right and good. Repentance is more than seeking forgiveness; it is seeking a right relationship with God. It is a critical part of the process of conversion.

In the first reading from the Acts of the Apostles, Peter scolded the people, saying, "God ... has glorified his servant Jesus, whom you ... denied in Pilate's presence ... You denied the Holy and Righteous One."

My first thought when reading this was: *Peter* said this? Isn't Peter the poster child for denying Jesus?

We should not judge Peter too harshly. He saw himself in the people who had denied Jesus. His own guilt is reflected in his words. In his own way, he was saying, "I understand why you did what you did. I made the same mistake."

He is well suited to share with them how to recover from their denial. His simple directive of "Repent, therefore, and be converted ... " was leading them to the next step.

Peter was calling them to repent, to establish a right relationship with God. He then invited them to open their hearts and pursue conversion.

The people's sin was denying Jesus. They must seek forgiveness and repent in an effort to set things right. Conversion will take place when they accept Jesus, when they believe.

When we confess our sins, two things take place. First, our sins are forgiven. Second, we are called to conversion.

In the *Catechism of the Catholic Church* we read, "Conversion is accomplished in daily life by gestures of reconciliation: concern for the poor, the exercise and defense of justice and right, by the admission of faults to one's brethren, fraternal correction, revision of life, examination of conscience, spiritual direction, acceptance of suffering, and endurance of persecution for the sake of righteousness. Taking up one's cross each day and following Jesus is the surest path to conversion."

Stated more simply, if our sin is selfishness, putting the needs of others first will lead us to conversion. If our sin is hatred, loving acceptance will lead us to conversion. If our sin is materialism, simplifying our lives will lead us to conversion.

The Easter season calls us to a conversion of our own: from unbelief to belief, from fear to courage, from doubt to certainty, separation from God to a right relationship with Him.

Connecting the conversion message to my earlier examples, for the children fighting, repentance is saying, "I'm sorry." Conversion is meaning it.

If I ever do have a disagreement with Carol, repentance will be apologizing in words. Conversion will be proving it by my actions.

Lent is about forgiveness and mercy. Easter is about repentance and conversion.

—April 2015

THE WALL ISN'T GOING TO PAINT ITSELF

Solemnity of the Ascension of the Lord   *Acts 1:1-11*
                                                Ephesians 1:17-23
                                                Mark 16:15-20

One early August day, my dad called for me to come out to the garage. I can't remember for sure, but I think I was around seven or eight years old.

Half of the garage had been completely emptied out, and there was plastic spread out on the floor. A metal pan, a roller, and a brush sat next to an open can of paint.

My dad handed me the roller and said, "You do this wall. I'll start over here."

That's it. That was the extent of my instructions.

It is important to note that I had never held a paint roller in my hand before that day. My previous painting experience included finger-painting in kindergarten and a paint-by-number book I got for First Communion.

My dad was a Marine, so the thought of questioning a direct order never crossed my mind. So I just stared at the wall and tried to decipher his somewhat vague painting instructions: "You do this wall."

I wondered if Dad had me confused with one of my three older brothers. I'm certain each of them had more painting experience than me. That happened with six kids in the house; Dad got us mixed up sometimes.

I stared at the wall a little longer. I was considering all my options when Dad stopped his own painting and asked, "Is there a problem?"

"I don't know how to paint," I told him.

I put down the roller, assuming he would come to his senses and remember I was just a little kid.

"Sure you do," he said.

"Remember last summer when I painted the living room and you asked if you could watch?"

I did remember that.

Then he said, "I told you it was okay to watch. I also told you to watch carefully because some day you would need to paint something yourself. Do you remember that?"

I did remember that.

"Today is that day," he said.

Then he went back to work.

I picked up the roller again and stared at the wall some more. I must have stared too long because Dad finally said, "The wall isn't going to paint itself. Get busy!"

As I reflected on today's scripture, I was reminded of my first painting experience.

In our first reading from the Acts of the Apostles, the two men in white garments asked the apostles, "Men of Galilee, why are you standing there looking at the sky?"

The scripture passage stops before we get to hear the response from the apostles. I'm sure they didn't actually say this, but I bet they were thinking something like this: "Why are we standing here looking at the sky? Because one minute we were talking to Jesus … and the next minute He was lifted up in a cloud and taken from our sight. We have no idea what to do next."

However, Jesus had given the apostles explicit instructions immediately before ascending. We heard those instructions in Mark's gospel: "Go into the whole world and proclaim the gospel to every creature."

He had *told* them, in very precise language, what to do next.

The men in white garments shared a sense of urgency on Jesus' behalf. What they were really saying was, "Don't just stand there staring at the sky. Get busy!"

Or as my dad might have said, "The world isn't going to proclaim the gospel to itself!"

It is not the first time we have heard such urgency from Jesus. After the resurrection, Mary Magdalene was standing outside the tomb, mourning the loss of her friend and Lord. Suddenly, she realized that the person she thought was a gardener was actually the risen Jesus.

She was overwhelmed and frozen in her tracks. She was unsure of what to do next. Jesus would have none of that. He said to her, "Stop holding on to me!"

He didn't want her to get caught up in the event but rather to focus on the work at hand. He wanted her to get busy.

Whether you're an inexperienced painter, one of the first apostles, or a close friend of Jesus, the message from Him is the same: "Get busy! Go about my work."

Here's the problem: As much as we want to obey Jesus' command to "proclaim the gospel to every creature," the task can seem overwhelming.

I had watched Dad paint. He had told me to watch carefully because I was going to need to paint someday. But the thought of actually doing it left me staring at the wall.

The apostles had watched Jesus in His ministry. He had told them to watch and learn because they were going to need to spread the gospel someday. But the thought of actually doing it left them staring at the sky.

We know our time is coming to do the work, but when it is actually in front of us, we feel unprepared. The sense of responsibility can be overwhelming. Instead of drawing on the lessons we've learned, our tendency is to dwell on the reasons that we cannot accomplish the task at hand: we're too young or too old, too inexperienced, too busy, or maybe ... too scared.

And when it comes to God's work? We do not feel worthy; we're not holy enough; or we're not comfortable sharing our faith with others.

In Paul's Letter to the Ephesians, he tries to give us the courage to stop staring and get busy. In his pep talk, Paul wrote: "Grace was given to each of us according to the measure of Christ's gift. And he gave some as apostles, others as prophets, others as evangelists, others as pastors and teachers, to equip the holy ones for the work of ministry, for building up the body of Christ ... "

Everyone has something to contribute. Someone spreads out the plastic, someone buys the paint, someone pours it in the pan, someone rolls the paint onto the wall.

We have all been given what we need to do the work of God, "each of us according to the measure of Christ's gift."

We have not been asked to do anything we are not capable of doing.

—◦◦◦◦—

We have a service hour requirement at school. We asked each of our seniors to write a reflection on his or her four years of service. One senior wrote, "I have realized that changing the whole world may be impossible for just one person, but I am fully capable of changing *someone's* world, and that's all that really matters."

I can't proclaim the gospel to every creature on my own, but I can do my share. I may not be able to paint the entire wall on my own, but every stroke of my paintbrush makes a difference.

So don't just stand there; the wall isn't going to paint itself.

—May 2015

ORDINARY TIME

BE THE VOICE

Solemnity of the Nativity   *Isaiah 49:1-6*
of John the Baptist 2012   *Acts 13:22-26*
                                       Luke 1:57-66, 80

The following homily is my very first homily, delivered the weekend of my ordination:

I was told by one parishioner, and I quote, "The most important thing about a homily is that it lasts seven minutes or less, and if it has a point, that's great too."

I will try to stay under seven minutes and do my best to have a point.

Today we celebrate the birth of John the Baptist. John is mentioned ninety-one times in the New Testament.

He was involved in some pretty dramatic events: He baptized Jesus in the Jordan and heard God speak. He was beheaded and his head served on a platter to King Herod.

We also know that John the Baptist was not a "mainstream" guy: He lived on the fringe of society. He was a desert dweller. He is described as wearing camel skin, having long scraggly hair and a beard, and it was written that he ate locusts and other insects.

Descriptions of John may conjure up an image of someone who is not quite "all there." But he is also described as "a voice crying out in the desert."

John had a powerful message that he was not afraid to share with whoever would listen. He preached a message of repentance. He was loud and somewhat "in your face," but the core of his message was one of love: be open to Christ, prepare for Christ, welcome Christ.

He was a voice crying out in the desert.

———

I work with an organization called HOOP (Helping Our Own People). Our work is simple: We stop at our storage facility and pick up clothing and toiletries. We stop at a local church and pick up soup, sandwiches, and fruit. Then we take these items out and distribute them to the homeless in downtown Indianapolis.

No questions asked. We just give them what they need and spend some time in conversation.

There is a deserted parking lot not far from Lucas Oil Stadium. A chain-link fence runs the length of the parking lot and separates the lot from a wooded area that slopes down to the river. Some of the fence has been cut away, allowing people to come and go through the opening. When you step through that fence, you step into another world: eight to ten tents and tarps serve as homes for up to twenty people.

On one particular night, we stopped and honked our horn to announce our arrival. People emerged to get food and whatever else we had to offer.

One of the regulars, Paul, did not respond. Thinking he might be asleep, I went through the fence and down the path to his "home." He was lying on a piece of plywood, with a tarp thrown over a branch to serve as his roof. He was covered with a thin sheet and a trash bag full of his worldly possessions sat next to him.

He lived on the fringe of society. He had a long scraggly hair and a beard. Seeing Paul may conjure up an image of someone who is not quite "all there."

I woke him up and told him HOOP had arrived. He sat up, stretched, and smiled. His first words were, "I am so blessed. God is good."

During our walk from his "home" back up to the car, he told me multiple times how blessed he was, how good God was, and how grateful he was that we were there.

Paul was always upbeat and positive.

After he ate and we spoke for a while, I told him that donors had been generous and that we had plenty of sweatshirts and blankets. It was going to be quite cold the next few nights. He told me that he was blessed and that he had everything he needed.

I tried again to get him to take some things, but he insisted that he had everything he needed. He said, "But I do have a favor to ask. There are a couple of new families who have moved in down by the river. Would you stop there and make sure they get everything they need?"

Like he always does, he ended by asking if I would join hands and say a prayer for him and his friends. On this night, I said, "Paul, you *are* so blessed. Would you pray for *me* and *my* friends?"

He smiled, we all joined hands, and Paul prayed for me and my friends.

Through his words and his actions, he is sharing a simple message of love: be open to Christ, prepare for Christ, welcome Christ.

Paul is a voice crying out in the desert.

—◆—

Take time to be still and listen to the voices crying out. They are inviting us to welcome Christ into our lives.

Be the voice. Through your words and actions, invite others to welcome Christ into their lives.

—Ordination Day, June 2012

WE HAVE BEEN GIVEN AUTHORITY

Fifteenth Sunday in Ordinary Time 2012   *Amos 7:12-15*
                                             Ephesians 1:3-14
                                             Mark 6:7-13

Part of the ordination rite a few weeks ago was what is referred to as "vesting." Candidates for ordination invite a priest to ceremoniously help them put on their new vestments for the first time. Since Fr. Jerry was my mentor for the first half of my formation and Fr. Jim served in that capacity for the second half, I invited both of them to be a part of my vesting. They both graciously accepted my offer.

It turned out to be a rather humorous event. Fr. Jim started things off by putting my stole over the wrong shoulder. Fr. Jerry followed up by putting on my dalmatic backwards.

Once I was *correctly* vested, my two-year-old grandson saw me standing there in my new attire and whispered to his mother, "Is grandpa a superhero?"

Mary responded, as every good daughter should, by saying, "Yes, Grandpa is a superhero!"

If you are an avid movie-goer, you must have noticed that the world seems to have a fascination with superheroes. In the last few years

DEACON RICK WAGNER

alone we have seen movies about Batman, Superman, the Avengers, Spider-Man, Iron Man, Thor, X-Men, Wolverine, Captain America, and more. Each of these bigger-than-life characters is equipped with multiple superpowers that they use to combat evil—to "drive out demons" if you will.

Which brings us to today's gospel, the initial sending out of the world's first superheroes, the apostles.

But these men present a much different image of a superhero. They did not possess any superhuman powers. Not only were these men not extraordinary, they were quite ordinary.

They were not the best and the brightest of the Jewish people, not even close. They were fishermen, tent makers, and tax collectors. They were run-of-the-mill men, damaged goods for the most part, broken men, sinners.

Yet here was Jesus, who had chosen this motley crew, sending these average men out to combat evil and sin. Not only were they not armed with special powers, they were not even given the basic necessities of travel: food, money, or a change of clothes. They had only the clothes on their backs and a walking stick.

Oh, but Jesus did give them one thing: "Jesus summoned the Twelve and began to send them out two by two, and gave them authority over unclean spirits."

He gave them authority—a strong faith and a dose of courage that gave them power over evil.

As His followers and as active members of His holy Church, we too are given authority. All of us—ordinary, unassuming, sinful people. Damaged goods for the most part, all of us have been given this authority.

So what am I supposed to do with it? "What good can one person do?"

130

A crowded locker room after gym class. Two boys begin to make comments about another boy, a small, shy boy who shrinks away. Another comment or two and now others begin to watch or join in. It happens in high school locker rooms everywhere.

We see the results on the news of how such a situation can blow up and do tremendous harm.

But on this day, a nondescript, ordinary boy—no bigger or stronger or more popular than any other boy—calmly steps into the mix and says loud enough for everyone to hear: "That's not how we are supposed to treat one another. This needs to stop." And it did.

He acted with authority.

"What good can one person do?"

An older man, who became known as Monon Bob, took a walk on the Monon trail every day. He stopped and talked to everyone he saw—runners, walkers, bikers. He carried a little black book with him and would make notes about the people he met. Even though he met hundreds, maybe thousands of people over time, he remembered their names and the names of their kids.

He took the time to get to know people. He would ask how someone's mother was doing after surgery or how the job search was going. When Bob died, the funeral home and church were overflowing.

Bob acted with authority.

"What good can one person do?"

As members of an apostolic Church, we are obligated to act to the extent that we are able. We may not be able to cast out demons, but ...

- We can do the right thing even when society tells us it doesn't matter.
- We can make the church stronger by being active in her ministries.
- We can invite our fallen-away Catholic friends back to the Church.
- We can involve ourselves in our community—putting our time, talent, treasure toward charitable work—and in so doing make life better for others.
- We can respond to injustice when we see it.
- We can live out the gospel message in word and deed.
- We can pray—pray in gratitude for our many blessings, pray for the needs of others, pray for the courage to use the authority given to us.
- We can, and must, integrate our faith into the secular world. Our faith cannot be something we put on for an hour on Sunday. It must be who we are. Our faith defines us.

We have been given authority.

We may not be able to eradicate unclean spirits, drive out all the demons, or wipe out evil overnight, but if we all answer our apostolic call, we can at least begin to tip the scales back in our favor.

—July 2012

THIS IS ENOUGH, LORD!

Nineteenth Sunday in
Ordinary Time 2012

1 Kings 19:4-8

Ephesians 4:30-5:2
John 6:41-51

In today's first reading, Elijah is tired.

We can feel his fatigue as we read, "Elijah went a day's journey into the desert, until he came to a tree and sat beneath it."

He said, "This is enough, Lord!"

Then he laid down and fell asleep. There is intensity in his tiredness. It goes far beyond the tiredness we feel after staying up too late to watch the Olympics.

If we go back several chapters in the book of Kings, we see that Elijah's fatigue was justified—years of having to survive drought and famine, hiding out in caves, caring for a widow and her son, bringing a child back from death, slaying 450 idolaters, and then once again fleeing for his life. Finally, he came upon this tree and collapsed beneath it.

He had relentlessly done everything God had asked of him with no time to rest. He was wiped out. He was done.

"This is enough, Lord!"

While I doubt that many of us can say we have endured all the hardships that Elijah faced, we can understand his fatigue. We know what it feels like to be so overwhelmed with stuff that we beg for it to stop—we want relief.

We want to say, "This is enough, Lord!" and lay down and just sleep.

It finally happened. We knew it was coming although we prayed it wouldn't. We were laid off from our jobs. Cutbacks had already taken away a portion of our income. It made living paycheck to paycheck impossible. Our savings is gone. Creditors continue to call. If we can't pay the electric bill by Friday, service will be cut off—again. What will we tell our spouse? We have been assuring them that everything would be okay. We're tired.

"This is enough, Lord!"

We struggle with addiction. We don't know how it got ahold of our lives. When did we lose control? We have turned away from everyone who loves us. We have been in and out of rehab. Four days is as long as we have been able to stay clean. Then the whole ugly cycle starts all over again. We never wanted this for ourselves. We see no light at the end of the tunnel. We're tired.

"This is enough, Lord!"

We spend years of our life caring for someone we love. Someone whose life is being drained by cancer or some other disease. Someone who was so alive now needs our help with the most basic skills—bathing, eating, dressing. We spend all our time caring for them. We get no relief, and there is no time to care for ourselves. We're tired.

"This is enough, Lord!"

Our kids are in pain, and it drives a knife into our heart. Their marriage is in trouble or their child is sick or they have turned away from the church. We feel their pain, but there is nothing we can do about it. We just lay in bed night after night worrying. We're tired.

"This is enough, Lord!"

Maybe these are your stories. Or there are countless other scenarios that could be bringing you to this point of mental and physical and spiritual exhaustion. Chances are good that we can all think of at least one time in our lives when we were at our limit.

When Elijah reached that point, he knew he needed rest and food to be renewed.

He slept in the shade of the tree and ate the food given to him by an angel of God.

Just as God had watched over him and provided for him so many times before, here He was again giving Elijah rest and food.

Scripture tells us repeatedly that God is encouraging us to seek rest too:

- "Be still and know that I am God."
- "My soul finds rest in God alone."
- "Come away by yourselves to a secluded place and rest a while."

Scripture also tells us repeatedly that God will provide all the nourishment we'll ever need.

We hear it in today's gospel when Jesus says, "I am the bread of life. I am the living bread that came down from heaven; Whoever eats this bread will live forever."

Just as it happened to Elijah, the world can sometimes close in on us and cause us to cry out, "This is enough, Lord!"

But it is worth noting the angel's final message to Elijah: "Once you have rested and eaten, you need to get back to doing the work of God."

So it is for us: God calls us to rest and to eat—and then get back to doing His work.

It is often said that having a strong faith means knowing that God is there for you—even during the tough times. Perhaps we can take it a step further: having a strong faith means knowing that God is there for you, *especially* during the tough times.

—August 2012

SNAKES DON'T HAVE ARMS

Thirty-first Sunday in Ordinary Time 2012

Deuteronomy 6:2-6

Hebrews 7:23-28
Mark 12:28-34

Snakes don't have arms.

That may not seem like something we need to spend much time debating, but as a five-year-old kindergartner back in 1964, this was a pretty big deal to which I devoted a great deal of time and energy.

There were lots of rules for my kindergarten class at John Strange Elementary:

- Don't push.
- Take turns.
- No running.
- Raise your hand to talk.

Even as a five-year-old, I was a rule follower, so I had no problem with these rules. As a matter of fact, I am proud to say that my adherence to the rules earned me the job of line leader on more than one occasion.

Classroom rules were not a problem for me. What was on the wall of the classroom was a problem.

As you walked into our classroom, there were pictures of three huge animals painted on the wall, each displaying a word or a phrase.

A polar bear was leaning up against an igloo, holding the words, "Be Nice." I knew that polar bears didn't live in igloos, but I could go along with the idea that he might occasionally pause to lean up against one.

A giraffe had the word "Share" balanced on his head. This bothered me *slightly* as I wondered how the word got there and how long it could actually stay balanced on his head, but I was able to get past that and accept it.

Finally, a snake was springing out of a coil, smiling and holding the words "Help Others." I could deal with the fact that the snake was smiling but not with the fact that he was holding something. Snakes don't have arms!

This bothered me. This bothered me a lot.

I had seen pictures of many different varieties of snakes, had been to the zoo and had seen live snakes, and none of them had arms.

I told my teacher that snakes don't have arms. She just smiled at me. I tried to tell some of my little friends that snakes don't have arms, but they didn't care. I didn't understand why this misinformation was being tolerated.

A polar bear leaning against an igloo—unlikely, but okay. Giraffes balancing stuff on their heads—okay, maybe. A snake smiling—a long shot, but I guess if he was happy enough, sure. But snakes do not have arms.

It was my mom who finally gave me something else to think about. I filled her in on what was going on at my terrible school, a place where they teach kids that snakes have arms. We needed to hold this school accountable for their gross malpractice.

Mom asked me, "What is the snake holding?"

This annoyed me. "Just some words."

"What do the words say?"

"I don't remember."

She knew.

"The words say, 'Help Others,'" she told me. "Maybe your teacher is trying to teach you that it is important to help others, *not* that snakes have arms."

I couldn't see the forest for the trees.

You might laugh at this story of a neurotic five-year-old, but as adults, we do this all the time, perhaps even daily.

Are petty thoughts and actions stealing away precious time? Is there an argument that has gone on much too long, perhaps so long you can't even remember how it started? Is your life cluttered with things you just need to let go?

We allow the minutia of life to take our focus off God's consistent message of love. I know that I often get so caught in the stuff of my life that I lose sight of what is really important; I lose sight of the message.

The scripture readings over the past several weeks have been focused on giving us instructions for living our daily lives. Last month, the rich young man proudly proclaimed that he had successfully followed the Ten Commandments and assumed he did all he needed to do.

Over the last week or so, the daily readings have been from St. Paul's Letter to the Ephesians, in which Paul states in no uncertain terms how people need to live their lives. Throughout Ephesians, we hear the following:

- "Children, obey your parents."

- "Fathers, don't provoke your children to anger."
- "Live in a manner worthy of the call you have received."

The Scriptures are full of life advice and references to rules, decrees, statutes, and commandments. All too often, we read them or hear them and perhaps even do our best to follow them while completely missing the message behind them.

It is like the new young driver who gets into the car on his own for the first time. He puts on his seat belt, adjusts his seat, adjusts his rearview mirror, and puts his hands at ten and two.

These are all necessary things, but something is missing. Oh yeah! The car keys!

With today's gospel, Jesus hands us the car keys.

We know life is more than following the Ten Commandments. After all, didn't we hear Jesus tell the rich young man that following the commandments is not enough?

Commandments, statutes, and decrees alone are not enough. They are just words without the unifying message that gives them life. The rules in kindergarten were not really about "not pushing" or "taking turns." They were about the unifying message: be nice, share, and help others.

The unifying message for us as Christians, the message that acts as the glue holding all God's rules together, is made clear to us in today's gospel:

> You shall love the Lord your God with all your heart, with all your soul, with all your mind, and with all your strength and You shall love your neighbor as yourself.

If you remember nothing else, just remember Jesus' simple words: "love God" and "love others."

This is how we should be spending our time. This is the unifying message that should act as a filter for all we do. Unfortunately, it is a message that often gets lost in the chaos and clutter of our lives.

It is the message we miss if we are too worried about whether or not snakes have arms.

—November 2012

NEXT MAN UP

Third Sunday in
Ordinary Time 2013

Nehemiah 8:2-6, 8-10

1 Corinthians 12:12-30
Luke 1:1-4, 4:14-21

In professional sports, there is an expression, "Next man up."

When you play in the NFL, everyone on the team practices every day. However, only the best eleven are on the field at any one time, so the others wait for their opportunity, never knowing if or when that time will come.

You hear the success stories all the time. A star player gets hurt and some guy no one has ever heard of steps onto the field, plays a great game, and leads the team to victory. He was the next man up, he was ready, and he responded.

Fear and doubt were there, but his joy, exhilaration, and preparedness allowed him to do the job he was called to do.

———

When couples exchange wedding vows at the altar, they promise to love one another in sickness and in health. The fact is, as they say those words, they are likely thinking it will never happen to them.

Then a long-term, debilitating disease comes along, and both are challenged—one by the disease itself, the other by the prospect of caring for her spouse, possibly for the rest of his life ... until death do they part.

One spouse can no longer care for himself. Maybe it's as simple as bringing him the remote or helping him out of the chair, but it might be more profound. He might need to be dressed and fed. She might need to be bathed, including fixing her hair just the way she likes it. They took the vows, they have had years to prepare, so when it happens, it's next man up.

I have had the privilege to witness loving couples go through such hardships. I saw how one spouse got past the fear and doubt and allowed love and a servant's heart to do the work necessary. They were not only living out their wedding vows; they were also living out the gospel message. Scripture was fulfilled in their actions.

There are times when I read a gospel passage that I wish I could have been there. I wish I could have been a fly on the wall in the synagogue in Nazareth the day Jesus was handed that scroll. He opened the scroll and read a Scripture passage from Isaiah: "The Spirit of the Lord is upon me, because he has anointed me to bring glad tidings to the poor." The gospel tells us, "The eyes of all in the synagogue looked intently at him."

There was electricity in the air. Something big was happening. Then Jesus said, "Today this Scripture passage is fulfilled in your hearing."

He basically told them, "What I just read is about *me*. It is happening right now. Christ is among you *right now*."

Can you imagine what must have been going through the minds of the people in the synagogue that day?

This man grew up right here in Nazareth. He's the man we've had our eye on because of all the odd things he has been doing—eating with sinners and tax collectors, healing on the Sabbath. This man is telling us He is the Christ.

I'm sure there was a whole range of thoughts and emotions coursing through the synagogue.

Fear: What if what he is saying is true? I have been waiting and preparing, but am I ready to meet Christ today?

Doubt: How can this be? I was expecting God's anointed one to ride in on a white horse, a king to save his people, not this simple preacher.

For some it may have been joy. Finally he has come! Praise God!

Jesus said, "Today this Scripture passage is fulfilled."

The word *today* is a powerful word. *Today* means there is no more time left, no more waiting: It's here. It's now.

In a very real sense, as we participate in Mass this weekend, and every weekend, this Scripture passage is once again "fulfilled in our hearing." The same Jesus who fulfilled the prophecies of Isaiah comes to us and is truly present to us in the Eucharist and in the Word.

How do we respond to that kind of news?

—◆—

In today's second reading, Paul writes to the Corinthians: "For in one Spirit we were all baptized into one body, now the body is not a single part, but many. *You are Christ's body.*"

If we are truly Christ's body, then Scripture is being fulfilled in *us* today.

When Jesus was in Nazareth, he was physically present. He himself served the poor, gave liberty to captives and sight to the blind, and sought to free the oppressed.

Today, he is physically present through us. We are the hands and feet of Christ.

We are the body of Christ. We are called to do the work of Christ on earth.

It is our responsibility now. We are the next man up.

We may be experiencing the same range of thoughts and emotions as the people did in the synagogue so many years ago.

Fear: Why me? Why today? What is the urgency?

Doubt: Am I really expected to do the work of Christ? How is that possible? I am not capable. I am not worthy.

Or joy: What a gift to be called upon to do God's work!

This news that we hear today, that Christ is among us and that we, His body, are called to do His work, brings us to a crossroads.

Which of these thoughts and emotions will we allow to direct us? Will we do nothing out of fear, panic keeping us frozen in our tracks? Will we be hesitant, allowing our doubts to convince us we are not capable of doing God's work? Or will we allow joy to bring us to full communion with Him, fearlessly taking on His work with a servant's heart?

Go ahead and take a minute to think about it, but don't delay too long. Scripture is being fulfilled by your actions today.

You're the next man up.

—January 2013

No Need to Pluck
Out Your Eyeball

Thursday of the Seventh Week   *Sirach 5:1-8*
in Ordinary Time 2013   *Mark 9:41-50*

This is some pretty graphic stuff Jesus is talking about: tying stones around our necks and getting thrown in the sea, cutting off hands and feet, and plucking out eyeballs.

It is certainly not the way we normally hear Jesus talk to His disciples. However, Jesus was an accomplished teacher, and He knew that sometimes He needed to shake things up a little bit to grab the attention of His audience.

What's really at the heart of these graphic examples? Jesus' point is really pretty simple: He wants us to identify what is it that is causing us to stray from the right path. He already knows what it is, but it is important that we discover it for ourselves.

What is keeping you from having the type of relationship with Jesus that both He and you would like to have?

What habits have you developed that steal away time that you could be spending with Jesus, time you could be spending on deepening your faith?

According to a 2010 study, Americans spend more than seven hours a day consuming media: watching TV, listening to music, surfing the web, social networking, playing video games, and using their cell phones to text, take pictures, or make calls.

If we take Jesus' words from today's gospel literally, perhaps we need to pluck out our eyeballs or cut off our texting fingers, or smash our computers and cell phones.

I don't think that is what Jesus is saying. I think He is simply asking us to remove some of the barriers.

Maybe we could take thirty minutes of those seven hours and give them to Him—to pray, to read Scripture, to sit in silence, or to serve others.

———

I see so many people—students, staff, and parents alike—entering the school each morning with a Starbucks or Dunkin' Donuts cup. We plan our entire morning routine around leaving enough time to get our coffee. We deal with morning traffic, wait in the drive-thru line, order the coffee, drive to the first window to pay, pick up our order, and get back into the morning traffic. On a good day, this is at least a ten- to twelve-minute exercise.

If we take Jesus' words from today's Gospel literally, perhaps we cut off the foot we use to press on the accelerator or slash the tires of our car.

I don't think that is what Jesus is saying. I think He is simply asking us to remove some of the barriers. Maybe one day a week we could skip the coffee run.

That would give us at least ten to twelve minutes once we arrive at school to sit in the chapel and spend time with Jesus.

———

The world tells us we need things to be somebody. We need the best of this or the newest version of that. This desire to have more and more things takes away from our relationship with God. Material things become idols to us.

We are in this world, but we do not need to be of this world.

If we take Jesus' words from today's gospel literally, perhaps we throw all our worldly possessions—our clothes and shoes and iPhones—into the fires of Gehenna.

I don't think that is what Jesus is saying. I think He is simply asking us to remove some of the barriers.

What are the things we no longer use? Can they be donated? Can the money that I was going to use to buy another outfit be spent on food to donate to the local food pantry?

In serving others, we serve God and enhance our relationship with Him.

———

Archbishop Tobin of Indianapolis, at one time a parish priest in Detroit, tells this story: Mother Teresa was visiting the United States and came to his parish. She needed a specific amount of money for a building project she wanted done. She made her appeal, and the parish responded. When the money was counted, she had collected just the amount she needed.

Archbishop Tobin, then Fr. Tobin, was disappointed, hoping that his parish would have been more generous and sent Mother Teresa home with **more** than she needed. He apologized to her that the parish wasn't able to do more for her.

Mother Teresa told him she was very pleased and did not want more than what she had asked for. She said, "If I have more than I need, it takes my focus off of God."

Jesus wants to be more important to us than Facebook or Starbucks or a new pair of shoes. He wants to be included in our plans for the day. He does not want to be an afterthought. He does not want to be the first thing cut from our day when our schedule gets too full.

We need to take a look at ourselves in the mirror and reflect on our part in our relationship with Jesus Christ. How one-sided has it become?

We must take the first step.

- Maybe the thirty minutes we take from our seven hours of media consumption will turn into forty minutes, then maybe an hour.
- Maybe the one day we skip our coffee to spend time in the chapel will become two or three days.
- Maybe we will learn from Mother Teresa that excess takes our focus off of God.

Jesus does not want us to pluck out our eyes or cut off our hands and feet, but he does want a part of us. He wants our time. He wants our attention.

How will we respond to His request?

—May 2013

JOB DESCRIPTION
OF A CHRISTIAN

Feast of Corpus Christi 2013   **Genesis 14:18-20**
                                      1 Corinthians 11:23-26
                                      Luke 9:11-17

Today is the Feast of Corpus Christi. The feast calls us to a true appreciation of the Eucharist, but it also calls us to focus on *this* body of Christ, us, the Church. In today's gospel, *Church* is fully alive, yet there is no building and no recited prayers.

Today we hear a familiar story: Jesus feeds five thousand people through the miracle of the multiplication of five loaves of bread and two fish. I have often wondered how the people present at such an event would have responded or how they would have perceived it. For example, what would the miracle have looked like through the eyes of the little boy who had the loaves and fishes?

My mom sent me to the market to get bread and fish. She gave me specific instructions: "Go right to the market and come right home." But on the way home, I noticed a crowd had gathered over on the hillside. A big crowd. Maybe I would just go over and check it out, just for a minute. Something drew me closer to the crowd and the unusual man talking to them. Another man spotted the package I carried and yelled, "This boy has food!" The unusual man prayed over my food and told others to pass it out. Then I watched it all happen. When it was all over, there was more food than I started with! Way more food! My heart was jumping out of my chest. It was a miracle! This man multiplied my loaves and fish and fed all these people! An even bigger miracle will be if I can avoid getting in trouble when I try to explain to my mom what happened.

Jesus was certainly capable of performing such a miracle, but I wonder if there was more to it. What else might have been going on? Were there other forces at work in the midst of the five thousand that day?

For example, I am part of the crowd and was asked to find a seat in the clearing.

I waited patiently to see how in the world they planned to feed all of us. There were people as far as I could see in every direction. I heard a couple of the disciples talking. All they had come up with was a few loaves of bread and a couple of fish. Word began to spread through the crowd: food was scarce. I was near the front of the crowd where they began to pass the food. I broke off a good size chunk of the bread and some of the fish. Then I broke off another piece of the bread to stick in my pocket for later. Who knew how much longer we were going to be out here?

But after I passed the food on, I looked up and saw Jesus and He locked eyes with me. I looked around and saw people who were likely much hungrier and more frail than me—women and small children, elderly folks. I probably didn't need that piece of bread I put in my pocket. So I broke it up and passed it behind me to others, who smiled and nodded at me. Come to think of it, I was not a big fan of fish anyway, so I broke my fish into pieces and passed it to the people in front of me. You know, it hasn't been that long since I ate, I would probably be fine if I didn't eat right now. I took the bread I still had and took it to the people near the back of the crowd. I broke up my remaining bread and passed it out—again, smiles and nods. Then I walked through the crowd, calling out to people, "If you can do without eating, please do. Pass it along to someone who needs it." I saw many people do just as I had asked.

Maybe this was not a "loaves and fishes" story at all, but people recognizing the need to look out for one another.

There are other possibilities. For example, the disciples went through the crowd, calling out and asking if anyone had any food to share. They got no response, so they tried again and again. Finally, they heard the voice of the little boy with the bread and fish. He offers the food graciously, without reservation. Upon seeing the charitable spirit of the young boy, some of the adults in the crowd open up bags and remove food they had with them and begin sharing it with others.

Maybe this was not a "loaves and fishes" story at all, but people seeing the value of a charitable spirit.

So what do we walk away with today? The incredible power of Jesus is on display, but I believe it goes beyond the miracle—the act of multiplying the loaves and fishes. People are hungry. They seek nourishment. They seek healing and consolation, forgiveness, and understanding. They are hungry for the Word. They are starved for compassion, and they long for a charitable spirit.

Jesus tells us, "Don't send them away. You feed them." Maybe we are the loaves of bread in the story, the bread that is being broken and passed among those who are hungry, the bread that provides nourishment to so many.

In the liturgical song "Christ, Be Our Light," verse three reads, "Longing for food, many are hungry. Longing for water, many still thirst. Make us your bread, broken for others, shared until all are fed."

Could it be that today's gospel is not a miracle story at all, but rather a job description of a Christian?

We must feed others. In so doing, we serve as both Eucharist and Church.

—June 2013

HUMILITY AND FREEDOM

**Thirteenth Sunday in
Ordinary Time 2013**

**1 Kings 19:16, 19-21
Galatians 5:1, 13-18
Luke 9:51-62**

I'd like to share a few thoughts on humility.

I recently stepped down as principal of Guerin Catholic High School after six years. There were several final events held, at which I was recognized for my years of service.

I was invited to be a speaker at the final Dad's Day Breakfast of the year. About four hundred people showed up, a much larger crowd than normal.

At the final all-school Mass of the year, the entire gymnasium was packed with students, parents, and board members, as well as the bishop. Before Mass began, I was in my vestments, leaning up against a wall, taking it all in.

All these people, I thought. *Here because of me, to hear me preach, and to thank me.*

The maintenance man, Ray, came and stood next to me. He looked at the crowd and said, "Man, this is a big crowd, biggest crowd we've ever had."

I nodded.

He said, "There was a huge crowd for your breakfast speech last week too."

Inside I was saying to myself, *I know! And it was all for me!*

Finally, Ray said, "Yeah, there sure are a lot of people excited to see you go."

Humility.

———

Now let's talk about freedom.

Freedom seems a relevant, if not hot, topic these days, especially on the heels of recent federal mandates and Supreme Court decisions. Soon we will enjoy the Fourth of July holiday, when we celebrate the freedom we enjoy in this country.

However, if you were to begin a conversation about freedom, you would find out quickly that there is no universal understanding of what the word *freedom* means.

I remember March Madness several years back. I was watching the late night news after the NCAA basketball championship game. A TV crew was on the campus of the winning team, reporting on the chaos that ensued following the game.

College students were running rampant, yelling and screaming. Fires were burning in trashcans. A couple of cars were flipped over. One student climbed to the top of a light post and was waving a school flag.

As this young man was being put in handcuffs by campus police, he turned to the news camera and said, "This is un-American! My great-grandfather fought in WWII to give me the freedom to do this!"

Really? That was the freedom your great-grandfather fought for? Well, that was one perspective on freedom.

I watched a documentary on the History Channel once that followed an immigrant from the time he came into the country until he became a naturalized citizen. For nearly five years, he worked fourteen hours a day, six days a week. He kept enough from his paycheck to pay for a small one-room apartment. The rest of his money was sent home to his wife and four children. He visited his family only a few times over the five years. On his one day off each week, he had a friend teaching him to read and write English and helping him study for his citizenship test. He lived a life most of us would consider very difficult, if not depressing.

When he was interviewed after being sworn in as an American citizen, he gave a big smile and said, "I love this country! A land of freedom and hope!"

Quite a different perspective on freedom.

—————

I think some people confuse freedom with entitlement. True freedom is not possible without humility.

Both Paul's Letter to the Galatians and today's gospel reading from Luke address the topic of freedom, of individual choice. They also speak to the fact that with freedom comes responsibility and the need for humility because often with individual choice comes hardship and sacrifice.

Paul wrote, "Christ set us free … use this freedom as an opportunity to serve one another through love."

He spoke of a freedom to be used not for our own selfish interests and desires but in service to others. We are called to humbly accept the freedom Jesus died to give us and do good in His name, making choices that glorify Him.

Today's gospel reminds us that opting for the right path, freely choosing to do good, can sometimes be quite challenging.

Jesus was approached by several people who had been listening intently to what He had to say. They asked Jesus if they could follow Him, if they could join Him on His journey. This was an admirable way to exercise their freedom.

He responded, "The Son of Man has nowhere to rest his head."

In other words, "Do you know what you are getting into? Are you prepared to do what it takes? To put aside your own wants and needs?"

Jesus' response might have sounded harsh, but it realistically illustrated the need to combine freedom with humility. One of the men he was speaking to accepted the challenge. The man said he was willing to accept the hardships that come with following Jesus.

Then he added, "But my father just died. Let me go and bury him first, then I will follow you."

Jesus responded, "Let the dead bury their dead. But you, go and proclaim the kingdom of God."

He does not affirm the man for his decision to follow Him or show compassion by allowing him time to bury his father. Instead he told the man, "If you're going to follow me, it must be now."

Many heard Jesus speak, but only a few freely chose to approach Jesus and ask to follow Him. This showed courage. They chose the right path. There is no more important work than the work of Jesus. It takes commitment, a commitment with no excuses.

Jesus asked them, "Are you in? Or are you out?"

Jesus asks us that same question. Are we in?

There is a sense of urgency in His question. He needs our help now more than ever.

Do we use the freedom we enjoy to satisfy our own desires or in humble service to others? Do we choose to take on the important work of Jesus even when it is not convenient?

To do the work of Jesus on earth, to proclaim the kingdom of God, requires humility.

Only a few step forward, and those that do realize that it will mean hardship and sacrifice. It will take courage.

In addressing this challenge, Pope Francis recently said, "Go on! Be courageous and go against the tide ... and be proud of doing it!"

—June 2013

HOARDING CHOCOLATES AND SHAMPOO

Eighteenth Sunday in Ordinary Time 2013

Ecclesiastes 1:2, 2:21-23
Colossians 3:1-5, 9-11
Luke 12:13-31

I hate to do this, but I need to talk for just a minute about some concerns I have for two of the women in my life. I thought long and hard about whether or not this is the appropriate forum to air this dirty laundry and have decided to move forward.

My wife, Carol, hoards chocolate.

She goes to the store and purchases groceries, including chocolate. Upon arriving home, she proceeds to hide said chocolate so that only *she* can enjoy it. This has been going on for years. I won't even mention the fact that others in the family have brought home chocolate that mysteriously comes up missing.

Next, my daughter Laura. She went through a phase during which she *refused* to share her shampoo. It was not shampoo that was specially formulated for only her. It did not come in a solid gold bottle. It was not the cheapest brand, but it was far from being the most expensive or even in the top ten.

The *only* reason she would not share her shampoo was that it was *hers.*

Quick story: Before she was married, she went on a vacation with her boyfriend's family. They paid for *everything* on this beautiful trip to Mexico. However, there were people on the trip who had the *nerve* to use Laura's shampoo.

The relationship survived, but right before the wedding, I whispered in the groom's ear, "Do *not* use Laura's shampoo."

The theme of today's readings is very clear: The message is about greed and a misplaced focus on earthly things that have no real value.

Paul tells the Colossians to "think of what is above, not of what is on earth."

We hear in Luke's gospel, "Take care to guard against all greed … one's life does not consist of possessions."

The movie *Wall Street* came out in the late 1980s. Michael Douglas starred as ruthless corporate executive Gordon Gekko. In one scene, while speaking at an annual stockholders meeting, he says, "Greed works. Greed is good."

The shareholders were mesmerized by Gekko, a millionaire who had all the riches any man could ever want. His argument made a lot of sense. If greed is what got him to that level of wealth, then greed *must* work. Since *they* wanted what *he* had and greed made it possible, then greed must be good. How could anyone argue with him?

Perhaps it is not greed that is the problem, but our definition of riches.

If riches mean lots of money, expensive toys, dining at the finest restaurants, buying whatever you want whenever you want it, or even keeping your chocolate or shampoo all for yourself, then greed is an excellent motivator.

For example: We say we want to provide our family with riches. So we take that promotion that means more travel, more responsibility, and more hours. We put in overtime and agree to work on Saturdays. We spend time returning e-mails and finalizing reports on Sundays. The paycheck comes, and it's bigger. We are able to buy nice things for our family and build up a nice bank account.

The more money we have and the more things we have, the more we want, or in our minds, the more we *need*.

Greed serves as our motivator, and we take advantage of every opportunity to work more, earn more, get more, and in turn, provide more. We have been effective in meeting our goal of providing riches for our family, *if* our definition of riches is having lots of stuff.

—⁂—

However, maybe we define riches as giving more of *ourselves* to our family:

- offering them the *richness* of our presence
- playing catch in the backyard and tucking the kids in at night
- having a cup of coffee and enjoying time with our spouse
- serving others together as a family
- being a living example to our children of what it means to be a loving, compassionate, moral, and humble human being

The goal of providing riches to our family is the same, but we have a different definition of riches.

Greed in this case would be ineffective.

—⁂—

160

Today's gospel warns us of the foolishness of greed. The rich man had so much grain that he decided to build bigger barns to keep it all for himself. He did that, only to find out that he would die that night.

What would all that wealth do for him then?

When you check in at heaven's gates, you won't be judged according to how many hours you worked, how much wealth you have, or how many *things* you have accumulated. You will be judged on the time you spent on earth in loving service to God and others.

Herein lies the problem with greed: While greed may enhance your focus and drive you toward your goal, the focus is misplaced and the goals have no real value.

Because greed draws your focus away from things of real value, it undermines true happiness.

—◦—

I remember seeing a black-and-white cartoon drawing many years ago. There were two cartoon panels side by side.

The first panel was the drawing of a Christmas shopping mall scene. The mall manager had opened the doors for the start of a business day and had been trampled and flattened under the feet of the thousands of shoppers rushing to get through the doors. He lay there on the ground with the keys still in his hand, a big smile on his face, and visions of dollar signs dancing in his head.

The second panel was a drawing of a sad parish priest, standing in front of open church doors, looking around for *anyone* who might be interested in coming to services.

Running the length of both panels was the caption "What if we were greedy *for God*?"

What a great question! What if we tried to accumulate prayer time like we try to accumulate wealth? What if we hoarded opportunities to serve like we hoard *things*? What if we were driven to love as much as we are driven to acquire?

I certainly don't want to see Fr. Jim get trampled, but what if we truly were "greedy for God"?

—August 2013

It's Worth Workin' For

Twenty-first Sunday in
Ordinary Time 2013

Isaiah 66:18-21
Hebrews 12:5-7, 11-13
Luke 13:22-30

I have a three-year-old grandson, a four-month-old granddaughter, and another grandchild due to arrive in January (three different families). One of the things I look forward to is the day when I can start giving my grandchildren advice. My own kids are grown up, so they don't listen to me anymore. It will be nice to have my grandchildren as a new audience for my wisdom and sage advice.

My Grandpa Jack was very good at giving advice, or at least he enjoyed doing it.

There was an arcade down the street from Grandma and Grandpa's house. When we would visit, Grandpa would have a list of jobs for us to do. If we did them, he would give us some change to go down to the arcade and play some games.

As we were working, we would of course complain, because that's what kids do when they work. Grandpa Jack had an expression he would use at those times. He would say, "If it's worth getting, it's worth working for."

That advice has always stuck with me. If you want it bad enough, you should be willing to work for it. We really wanted to go to the arcade, so doing all those jobs for Grandpa was worth it.

———

Grandpa Jack's words came back to me as I read today's scripture passages.

In the Letter to the Hebrews we hear, "Endure your trials as discipline; all discipline seems a cause not for joy but for pain, yet later it brings the peaceful fruit of righteousness."

And in Luke's gospel, we read, "Strive to enter through the narrow gate, for many, I tell you, will attempt to enter but will not be strong enough." And the final line from the gospel is "For behold, some are last who will be first, and some are first who will be last."

When we put these two readings together, the message seems quite clear: We must put in the work. We must persevere. Or as Pope Francis has told us, "Swim against the tide; it's good for the heart, but it takes courage."

When we do these things—put in the work, persevere, and swim against the tide—we earn the gift of eternal life.

But it's not that simple, is it? The work is difficult. It never lets up. The tide of society that we must swim against is very strong.

Society says do what feels good. God says do what is pleasing to Him.

Society says serve yourself. God says serve others.

Society says live in the moment. God says live for eternal life.

You get the idea. Society offers the easier path. We can wear ourselves out just trying to do the right thing when there are so many options that are easier. It can really begin to eat away at us.

———

I know I have spoken of this in previous homilies, the concept of Jesus "locking eyes" with us. That phrase captures how I feel when I suddenly realize I am heading down the wrong path. I see an image of Jesus taking my head in His hands and locking eyes with me.

He doesn't need to say a word. His look alone tells me that I need to refocus and get myself back on track.

There are days that we feel drained, wiped out, worn out from keeping God's work as the priority in our lives. On those days, we want to take Jesus' head in *our* hands, look *Him* in the eyes and say, "I can't do this anymore. It's too much. I am overwhelmed. The cross you have given me is too heavy."

Why can't we let up sometimes? Why can't we relax? Why do we have to *earn* everything we get? Why can't we just go to the arcade sometimes *without* working for it?

We *want* to tell Jesus, "We don't know what you want from us! We don't understand what we are being called to do."

We are working so hard to be good parents. The kids get older, but parenting never seems to end. No matter their age, we are always worried about them, their lives, their decisions, and the strength of their faith.

We have aging parents who need us. They gave so much to us growing up; we know we need to help them. We love them, but they need more than we can give. It never ends.

We are constantly worried about money. Will we have enough to pay the bills this month? We are working as much as we can, but there never seems to be extra.

We find ourselves getting weaker and tempted to go down the wrong path. We don't feel strong enough to swim against the tide much longer.

All this is going on in our lives, yet our faith calls us to give *even more*. There is only so much time and so much love to give, and we feel tapped out.

We *want* to tell Jesus all of these things. We *want* to let it all out, but we don't. We fear Jesus will reject us or see us as weak.

Well, here's a news flash: Jesus already knows we are weak.

He *wants* us to come to Him with our struggles. He *wants* us to unload on Him. He locks eyes with us when we lose focus and become self-centered. But when we tell Him we are feeling vulnerable and depleted, He pulls us into His loving arms.

He calls us to "come away and rest awhile." He tells us that He will take on our burden. He assures us that others will step up too; others will be our Simons of Cyrene.

And when we have had the time we need and taken our rest, He will again lock eyes with us and tell us, "It's time."

Then we will pick up our cross and get back to work because we know it is the right thing to do. Refreshed and renewed, we may even see others around us who are feeling overwhelmed. They now are saying to Jesus, "I can't do this anymore!"

When we see that, we go to them and see what we can do to help lighten *their* load.

And so the journey continues for a disciple of Christ. Doing the work of God is difficult, but the payoff is worth it.

Or as Grandpa Jack said, "If it's worth getting, it's worth working for."

—August 2013

LUMP

Twenty-fourth Sunday in   *Exodus 32:7-11, 13-14*
Ordinary Time 2013   *1 Timothy 1:12-17*
                          Luke 15:1-32

There is a series of short Christian-based videos narrated by Rob Bell and produced by a company called NOOMA. One of the videos is called *Lump*.

In the video, Mom was cleaning the kitchen while two young boys, maybe four and six years old, were playing in the next room. She found a small rubber ball in the "junk bowl" where all the odds and ends of life seem to land—paper clips, rubber bands, batteries, a couple of pens, and a few stray pennies.

She had never seen the rubber ball before and was curious where it came from. So she called her two boys into the kitchen. She held up the small ball and said, "Do either of you know where this came from?"

The four-year-old immediately said, "Nope!" and jumped into the air, made a goofy noise, and ran off to play. Meanwhile the six-year-old was frozen, the life draining from his face. He talked quickly, "No, I don't know where it came from. It's the strangest thing. A little rubber ball. Where could that have come from? It's the strangest

167

thing. It's like it just appeared. I have no idea where that rubber ball came from. It's the strangest thing."

He had not moved an inch, and he had a very uncomfortable smile on his face. This went back and forth, with Mom asking a few more questions, and her son being *overly* animated and *overly* amazed at the ball that had magically appeared.

Mom was on to him, but she let him sweat. Ultimately, she called him on it, indicating that she knew he took the ball from some-where—maybe from a friend without asking or from a store without paying.

Think back to when you were a child. Remember how you felt when you realized you were busted. The boy ran upstairs.

Dad arrived home two hours later. Mom filled him in on the story and indicated that she had not seen the boy since he ran upstairs.

Dad went upstairs and checked the boy's room. Not there. Looked in his brother's room and the bathroom. Not there. Finally Dad opened the bedroom door of the parent's room. There, in the middle of Mom and Dad's bed, under the covers, was a lump. The lump was breathing, but it was not moving.

Dad pulled back the covers to reveal his six-year-old son, soaked in sweat and trembling. He scooped up the lump, held him in his arms, and sat on the edge of the bed. The boy began to cry. He sobbed with deep breaths. He was not saying a word, just crying as his Dad pulled him in tight to his chest and squeezed him in his arms.

Dad began to stroke his son's hair and rocked him back and forth. Then Dad said over and over again, "There is nothing you could ever do to make me love you less. There is nothing you could ever do to make me love you less. There is nothing you could ever do to make me love you less."

We hear this very same story in the gospel today. In the parable of the prodigal son, the young son demanded his inheritance and struck out on his own. He rejected his father and the life he had been given. It was all about *him*.

He spent every last dime on wastefulness and excess. It was not until he hit rock bottom that he realized—he was busted. He became the lump.

I have read and heard this parable so many times. I have discovered that there is one word that makes the entire parable of the prodigal son come alive for me. A three-letter word that gives deeper meaning to the whole story.

It is the word *ran*.

Luke 15:20 reads, "While he was still a long way off, his father caught sight of him, and was filled with compassion. He *ran* to his son, embraced him and kissed him."

The father didn't wait for his son to get closer. He didn't send one of his servants out to greet him. He didn't *walk* to his son. He *ran* to his son, embraced him, and kissed him.

His son had rejected him, taken half his money, and wasted all the money on wild living. Yet the father *ran* to his son.

The father *rejoiced*, saying, "This son of mine was dead, and has come to life again; he was lost, and has been found."

With the video in mind, I picture the father holding the prodigal son tightly, rocking him back and forth, and saying, "There is nothing you could ever do to make me love you less."

Total and unconditional love. Therein lies the hope found in today's gospel message: There is nothing *we* could ever do to make *God* love us less. *Nothing*.

God is saying this to us over and over. What is keeping us from hearing it?

God is running to us. What is keeping us from allowing Him to pull us into his loving arms?

Perhaps it is shame. A dark offense that we are too ashamed to bring to him. Something we don't talk about to family or friends. Something we keep hidden, and the shame is eating away at us.

There is nothing we could ever do to make God love us less.

Maybe it is a sense of unworthiness. God couldn't possibly love us because we are unlovable. We have fallen over and over again. We are broken and unsalvageable.

There is nothing we could ever do to make God love us less.

Or maybe it is fear. Fear of the unknown. Fear of totally committing to God. Fear of being pulled into His arms and relinquishing all control over to Him.

There is nothing we could ever do to make God love us less.

Reconcile with yourself. Reconcile with God. Say to Him, "I have sinned against you."

Reconciliation is simply allowing God to run to you. Allowing Him to take you in His arms and rock you gently. Allowing him to say, "There is nothing you could ever do to make Me love us less."

You're busted. Now what?

You may be a lump, but you don't have to stay a lump.

—September 2013

Stir into Flame the Gift of God

Twenty-seventh Sunday in Ordinary Time 2013

Habakukk 1:2-3, 2:2-4
2 Timothy 1:6-8, 13-14
Luke 17:5-10

The readings for today offer a rich variety upon which to reflect. To be honest, this was a difficult week to prepare a homily—not because there was nothing to sink my teeth into, but because there was *so much* from which to choose.

The first reading looks at the age-old question: Why is there so much violence and ugliness in a world created by God? It reads, "Destruction and violence are before me. Why do you let me see ruin? Why must I look at misery?" One only needs to watch the evening news to begin to ask those same questions.

The gospel has *two* great themes: One image is that of the power of faith, even if only the size of a tiny mustard seed. A second image is that of the unprofitable servant, who must do the work of God without expectation of reward or even time to rest.

But each time I read, I kept coming back to one line from Paul's Second Letter to Timothy, "Stir into flame the gift of God."

I like camping and being in the great outdoors, but I would not consider myself a survivalist. There is a show on the Discovery Channel that follows a survivalist as he takes on all that a particular rugged landscape has to offer. A helicopter drops him down into the rain forest or the mountains or a frozen tundra and leaves him there for a week to test his survival skills.

It becomes very clear each time I watch this show that regardless of the environment the survivalist finds himself in, his survival ultimately hinges on fire.

Not only his ability to *start* a fire, but also to keep it going. A campfire left untended will die out.

The survivalist knows that he must occasionally stir the embers, fan the flame, and feed the fire in order for it to continue producing the desired heat.

Paul references this survival technique when he writes, "Stir into flame the gift of God."

He is not referring to a campfire, however. He is talking about the flame of the Holy Spirit, the fire of our faith. We recall that John the Baptist said of Jesus: He will baptize you with the Holy Spirit and fire.

That fire, a gift from God, can also die out if left untended.

Like a survivalist's campfire, we need to stir the embers, fan the flame, and feed the fire in order for our faith to survive.

—⸙—

My mom died at the much too early age of forty-three. It happened suddenly and unexpectedly, and just that quickly, she was taken from my dad, my five siblings, and me.

I was a fifteen-year-old at the time, and my teenage faith was already tenuous. When I added anger at God and an unanswered why to the situation, the weakened flame of my faith was in real danger of going out.

The Holy Spirit, a gift from God never to be taken away, was still there but was dormant from lack of use, from lack of passion, and from lack of faith.

The embers needed to be stirred, and the flame needed to be fed. That was not going to happen on its own, and I was in no condition to do it myself. I was an unskilled survivalist dropped into unchartered territory with no idea how to get a flame started.

Luckily I had people in my life who reached out to me. They refused to let me go down the wrong path. People saw what was happening and did their best to stir into flame my dying faith.

Paul gave Timothy the directive, "Stir into flame the gift of God."

He intended his message to have two meanings. First, do what is needed to keep the Holy Spirit alive in your heart, the flame of your faith alive. *Stir the embers* by loving God and others. *Fan the flames* by being the unprofitable servant, serving God and others without expectation of earthly reward. *Feed the fire* with prayer and evangelization.

Secondly, Paul was encouraging Timothy to stir into flame the fires of others when he saw them dying out. Watch for those whose flame may be smoldering and help bring them back to life.

—⁂—

I have been amazed more than once by that survivalist on TV, who would return to his camp after being out on some adventure for one or two days. He would look at his campfire, from all appearances completely burnt out, and say something like, "I needed to see if my fire had any life left in it."

I would think to myself, "You've been gone for two days. Of course there is no life left in it!"

Sometimes the fire would indeed be completely out. Other times, he would kneel down, take a stick, and begin to stir the embers. He would notice the tiniest red glow, perhaps even the size of a mustard seed, down in the ashes. He would bend down and blow on that weak ember, and it would glow brighter. Then he would grab some brush and some wood shavings and feed that glow, still blowing on it to resuscitate it. Eventually the flame would pop, the brush would catch fire, and moments later, there would be a roaring fire.

A fire that looked dead was restored to its full heat-producing capability.

What kind of world could we create if we were deliberate in our efforts to keep the flame of the Holy Spirit burning in our own hearts? What kind of world would it be if we each tried to fan one another's flame of faith? If the Holy Spirit was alive and well in *all* our hearts? Maybe a world with less of the violence and destruction mentioned in today's first reading.

Pope Francis recently said, "The Holy Spirit is giving people the good news that God loves them and can renew, purify, and transform their lives."

We cannot allow such a gift to die. We must do our part to stir it into flame.

—October 2013

NO LAMPSTAND REQUIRED

Fifth Sunday in Ordinary Time 2014   *Isaiah 58:7-10*
1 Corinthians 2:1-5
Matthew 5:13-16

The theme of today's readings is clear. The message we hear is about *light*—our light and our ability to shine that light, to share that light with others.

From the prophet Isaiah we hear, "Then your light shall break forth like the dawn." And from Matthew's gospel, we hear, "You are the light of the world."

We are also presented the image of a lamp being set on lamp stand, where it can give light to all in the house. It is a powerful image and one of my favorite Gospel passages.

I have used this image many times when giving talks to young people on leadership retreats. I impress upon them that God gives each one of us incredible gifts, and we have an obligation to share those gifts, to let them shine brightly for all the world to see.

If you have a beautiful voice, you need to sing. If you have artistic ability, you need to draw, paint, or sculpt something beautiful to share with the world. If you are gifted academically, you need to put those gifts to work. If you have leadership gifts, then you need to lead.

If you do not share these gifts, if you hide them under a bushel basket, you are being selfish. You would be rejecting a gift from God. This is powerful message.

However, when I read the gospel this time, within the context of the other readings, another message emerged. I wonder if my focus has been too narrow in the past.

I still believe that we are called to share our God-given gifts, of course, but the *source of the light* is in question. Does it come from us? From our gifts?

I think the light Isaiah and Matthew refer to is not our light; it is the light of Christ shining through us, and that opens up new possibilities.

What are those possibilities? It would mean that even if I wasn't given the gift of a beautiful voice, I could choose to sing anyway and allow the light of Christ to shine through me.

If I wasn't given the gift of artistic ability, I could create anyway and allow the light of Christ to shine through me.

If I wasn't given great academic gifts, I could choose to work hard and study right alongside my more gifted classmates and allow the light of Christ to shine through me.

The light of Christ is not intended to simply bounce off our God-given gifts and radiate out to the world. Rather, it is intended to shine through us and reflect both who we are and who Christ is to others.

I coached CYO football here at St. Pius for a number of years. I was fortunate one year to receive an award from the CYO for my years of coaching youth.

We went to St. Philip Neri for Mass and the award ceremony. The archbishop at the time was Archbishop Edward O'Meara.

At the end of the Mass, all the award recipients, maybe twenty of us from all over the Archdiocese, got in line alphabetically to receive our awards. Of course, I am a *W*, so I was near the back of the line.

As I got closer, I could hear the archbishop saying the same thing to each recipient. He said, "Thank you for your efforts, but your work is not yet done." Even though he said the same thing to every other person, I felt like he was speaking directly to me. He handed me my plaque, shook my hand, and looked me square in the eye, and said, "Thank you for your efforts, but your work is not yet done."

It gave me chills and at the same time made me uncomfortable.

What work was not done? Coaching? Helping CYO? Working with youth?

His face and those words stayed with me for years. As a matter of fact, he appeared in many of my dreams. Sometimes he would have a speaking part and say those same words to me, "Thank you for your efforts, but your work is not yet done." Then he would wave or smile. Other times he didn't speak at all but would just show up in my dream and look at me.

It didn't matter if my dream took place on a football field, at the grocery, or on an airplane, Archbishop O'Meara would be there, fully vested and smiling.

I remember one dream in particular. We had two young children at the time. In the dream, Carol and I loaded everyone in the station wagon (one of those cool ones with wood on the side) to go somewhere.

I needed to back the car out of the driveway, so I looked in the rear-view mirror. There, sitting between my two kids in their car seats, was Archbishop O'Meara, miter and all.

I did not seem caught off guard by this. I acted as though it was a normal occurrence. I nodded and said, "Archbishop."

He nodded back and smiled. I said, "Could you take off your hat? I can't see to back up."

He said, "Sure," and took off the miter. Then he said, "Thank you for your efforts, but your work is not yet done."

———

As I prepared the homily for this weekend, the archbishop dreams popped back into my head. I spent a considerable amount of time trying to figure out why.

This is what I came up with: When Archbishop O'Meara said, "Thank you for your efforts," he was acknowledging that I was sharing my God-given gifts.

I was allowing my light to shine just as those with beautiful voices or artistic talent do. My gifts were my gifts to use or not use, to put on a lamp stand or hide under a bushel basket. If I used them, I was to be commended. But that wasn't enough, so he told me, "Your work is not yet done."

I needed to be open to allowing *Christ's* light to shine through me.

We all need to be open to it. We need to reach beyond our obvious gifts, climb out of our comfort zones, and step into unchartered waters. If we don't, our work is not yet done.

If we do, we are likely to discover that our greatest gift is to be a gift to others.

Isaiah spells it out for us: "Share your bread with the hungry, shelter the oppressed and the homeless; clothe the naked when you see them, and do not turn your back on your own. Then your light shall break forth."

In a later chapter in the Gospel of Matthew, Jesus encourages us to share the gift of service when he says, "Whatever you do for the least of my brothers, you do for me."

Serving others, and charitable thoughts and actions, don't require special talents, but they do require that we be open to allowing Christ's light to shine through us.

No lamp stand required.

—February 2014

Did God Set Us Up to Fail?

Fourteenth Sunday in
Ordinary Time 2014

Zechariah 9:9-10
Romans 8:9, 11-13
Matthew 11:25-30

A question came to mind as I heard St. Paul's Letter to the Romans: did God set us up to fail?

I certainly don't want to second-guess God, but at times, what He asks of us and the position He puts us in do not seem to be in alignment. I am sure you have heard the expression, "Put yourself in a position to succeed." The implication is that we should do things that accentuate our gifts and talents, that allow us to use our strengths while diminishing our weaknesses.

We follow that logic at school. We schedule students into classes based on their academic abilities and strengths. We put teachers in front of them who are licensed and competent in the subject matter, in the hope that the students experience success. We wouldn't put a freshman student who struggles in Math into the highest level Calculus class or assign a teacher to the class who is trained to teach Social Studies. We would be setting that student up to fail.

I shared a story a few weeks ago about a fictional Fr. Joe, who did not prepare at all before attempting to deliver a homily. He was set up to fail, and he did just that.

Which brings me back to my original question: Did God set us up to fail?

In Paul's Letter to the Romans, he distinguishes between being "in the flesh" and "in the spirit," saying, "You are not in the flesh; on the contrary, you are in the spirit … if you live according to the flesh, you will die, but if by the Spirit … you will live."

What does Paul mean when he says "in the spirit"?

He means that God created us in His own image and breathed life into us, giving us the gift of the spirit and confidence that God is present in our lives. Thus, we are "in the spirit."

Yet we also have a sinful nature. We are imperfect creatures who are easily tempted and prone to poor judgment.

Then God takes us, His "in the spirit," sinful creations who are prone to exercise poor judgment, and drops us into a temporal world, which very much "in the flesh."

What does Paul mean when he says "in the flesh"? He means we live in a world that is of the world:

- A world in which people are consumed by what makes them feel good, with little regard for consequences
- A world focused on acquiring "things," chasing after material possessions that go far beyond basic human need
- A world in which people are objectified for the personal pleasure of others
- A world in which beauty is defined by appearances rather than value
- A world in which the needs of others are someone else's problem

This "in the flesh" world is a shortsighted world, concerned only with the here and now, with no regard for eternal life. It is empty and shallow and unfulfilling. Paul tells us that this world comes with a warning: "if you live according to the flesh, you will die."

If you live by the rules of the world, you die by those same rules. You die empty and unfulfilled. *This* is the world into which God has placed us.

Ironically, the "in the spirit" human beings into whom God breathed life are the ones who created the "in the flesh" world. He had to have seen that coming. Did He set us up to fail?

I could answer that question by saying, "Yes, God set us up to fail" and send you all home depressed and hopeless. I won't do that.

If we really thought God wanted us to fail, we would need to believe two things:

1. That He gave us *none* of the gifts, talents, or skills needed in order to take on the world and overcome its negative effects
2. That He offers us no additional resources, nothing that we can rely on for assistance when times are tough

Clearly, neither of these things are true. God not only gave us the aforementioned spirit breathed into us at Creation, but He also endowed us with the gift of free will. It is free will that allows you to say, "I have a choice."

You do not have to accept the world as it is. You do not have to surrender to its fleshiness or fall into the hopelessness that so many people allow to control their lives. You can choose not only to avoid the pitfalls of this world but also to be an agent of change. You can choose to make a difference.

There are others just like you who do not want to be swallowed up by an "in the flesh" world. You are not alone.

As for the idea that God offers us no additional resources, there is nothing further from the truth. There are at least two undeniable resources always at our disposal.

First and foremost, God Himself serves as a resource. He offers Himself to us on an as needed basis, and He is always open for business.

In Matthew's gospel today, we heard, "Come to me, all you who labor and are burdened, and I will give you rest."

In our uphill battle against an "in the flesh" world, we will likely grow tired and weak. We may also feel alone. It is comforting to know that we can turn to God when we are burdened, and He will give us rest. He will allow us to rest and recuperate before heading back into battle.

The second resource extended to us is forgiveness. In every battle, there are casualties. Remember, we are imperfect, sinful creatures. We will stumble at times and fall victim to the fleshiness of this world. When we do stumble, that does not have to be the end. We do not need to be permanent victims.

With rest and forgiveness, we are strengthened and reconciled to the spirit. And when we live "in the spirit," we have the hope of eternal life.

In 33 AD, Jesus commissioned His apostles—a small group of fisherman, farmers, and tax collectors—to take the gospel message out to the world. The world at that time was "in the flesh" just as it is today. These men were untrained and unqualified. They were sinful and stumbled countless times along the way, even denying that they knew Jesus.

Despite all of this, there are nearly 2.2 billion Christians in the world today. Were the apostles set up to fail?

God gives us life "in the spirit" and the gift of free will. God offers us rest and forgiveness. He has put us in a position to succeed.

—July 2014

WHY IS GOD EATING
LUNCH AT MCDONALD'S?

Eighteenth Sunday in   *Isaiah 55:1-3*
Ordinary Time 2014   *Romans 8:35, 37-39*
                                           Matthew 14:13-21

A little background before I share a story: When our children were young, Carol and I would prepare them before walking into Sunday Mass here at St. Pius. We would remind them that we were entering the house of God and that they all needed to be on their best behavior. We added that if they were quiet and really listened, God would talk to them.

Our two daughters paid close attention to what we said and were generally well-behaved and attentive. Not so much with the boys. They didn't really care whose house it was; they were going to do whatever they wanted.

And now the story: We were having lunch in McDonald's one afternoon. Mary, our oldest, was about four years old.

The pastor of St. Pius at that time was Fr. Jim Sweeney. Long-time parishioners will remember Fr. Jim as a big man with a big personality. He knew no strangers, and you always knew when Jim Sweeney was around.

He walked into that same McDonald's that afternoon. After ordering, he walked around the restaurant, waving to parishioners and stopping to chat at most of the tables, including ours.

Mary could not take her eyes off him. She was mesmerized. When Fr. Jim moved on to the next table, Mary leaned over to Carol and me and asked, "Why is God eating lunch at McDonald's?"

<hr />

Today I will be talking about God and food—or more precisely, God and being fed.

Through the prophet Isaiah, God tells us:

- "… receive grain and eat"
- "… drink wine and milk!"
- "… eat well"
- "… delight in rich fare"

And in the Gospel of Matthew, we hear the familiar story of the multiplication of the loaves and fishes. While initially there was concern about the five thousand going hungry, later in the story we are told, "They all ate and were satisfied, and they picked up the fragments left over—twelve wicker baskets full."

Food is mentioned in both scripture passages but not just subsistence food. Not the bare minimum to get by, but abundance! Free-flowing milk and wine! Twelve wicker baskets full!

Why this emphasis, in both the Old and New Testament, on food? No one likes a good meal more than me, but surely God does not have my lunch menu on the top of His priority list.

These readings that speak so much about food have little to do with eating, and everything to do with being fed. It is important to note who it is that is being fed.

From Isaiah, we read, "Thus says the Lord: All you who are thirsty … who have no money, come, receive grain and eat; Come, without paying and without cost."

As for those who were among the five thousand, the gospel tells us, "When Jesus disembarked and saw the vast crowd, his heart was moved with pity for them."

The people being fed, being nourished, were not simply a group searching for a unique dining experience. The people being fed were depleted, hopeless, to be pitied. They were searching for something. They needed to be fed.

We know what that feels like, don't we? Because we've been there. Or perhaps we are there now.

We need to be fed, yet what we take in doesn't satisfy us. We find no free-flowing milk or wine, and our wicker baskets are not full. We encounter scarcity or emptiness rather than abundance.

We need to take a hard look at what food line we are standing in. To whom or to what are we turning to be fed?

While there is much to be gained from reflecting on our own hunger, the message we hear today is one of hope, one of joy.

Four times in Isaiah, we hear the Lord inviting us, literally begging us, to come to Him:

- "Come to the water!"
- "Come, receive grain and eat …"
- "Come, without paying and without cost …"
- "Come to me heedfully …"

God invites us over and over again into his loving arms to be fed.

In the gospel, the five thousand were not fed because they happened to be in the right place at the right time. The five thousand were fed because they followed Jesus. They were hungry and turned to the One who could truly nourish them.

The miracle that day had nothing to do with loaves or fish. The miracle occurred as soon as they left their homes to follow Jesus.

Paul's Letter to the Romans captures the essence of the theme that runs through all of today's readings: "Neither death, nor life, nor angels, nor principalities, nor present things, nor future things, nor powers, nor height, nor depth, nor any other creature will be able to separate us from the love of God."

Nothing can separate us from the love of God. *Nothing* can separate us from the love of God. Nothing.

He tells us to come to Him. What He feeds us will satisfy. The love of God is free-flowing. It fills our wicker basket hearts. What we seek in other places, God offers us in abundance.

At a time when newspapers are full of stories of hopelessness and godlessness, pause for a moment to envision a world in which everyone turned to God to be fed.

Once fed, once nourished, we will have the strength to feed others. As Jesus suggests, we can "give them some food ourselves." Imagine the hope and the joy that would be found in such a world. God's presence would be felt everywhere. He would *be* everywhere. We may even find Him eating lunch at McDonald's.

—August 2014

Standing Off to the Side

When I am preparing to preach, I study the readings for the weekend several times, highlighting words and jotting down notes as I go.

This week I highlighted two passages: From Paul's Letter to the Romans, "I urge you ... to offer your bodies as a living sacrifice." And from Matthew's gospel, I highlighted, "Whoever wishes to come after me must deny himself, take up his cross, and follow me."

So we have "offer your body as a living sacrifice" and "deny yourself" and "take up your cross." Next to these highlighted passages, I wrote, "Jesus needs a new marketing team."

Hearing these passages wouldn't cause many people to say, "Christianity sounds great. Where do I sign up?"

Being a disciple of Christ can be a pretty tough road at times. It's not surprising so many veer off the road or choose a different road altogether, opting for the path of least resistance.

—————

Carol and I have four children, two boys and two girls. Growing up, the two boys could not have been more different. My son Rick was an athlete. He always had a ball in his hand. He would play football, then basketball, then baseball, then repeat the cycle all over again.

Coaches who had Rick on their team loved him because he was considered a "coachable kid."

Which simply meant, he would follow directions and do what he was asked with no questions asked. A coachable kid would run through the wall for his coach.

Robby, not so much. He was not an athlete and never really wanted to be an athlete. He went out for football in fifth grade because he thought that was what he was supposed to do. His friends played football, his brother played football, his dad coached football, so he figured he should give it a shot.

One of Robby's coaches shared this story with me. At practice, the team was doing a drill called The Pit. Two players would line up across from one another, and on the coach's whistle, they would collide and try to move the other backward while the rest of the team cheered them on. Barbaric, of course, but it was fun, and it gave the coaches an idea of how their new, young players would respond to hitting and being hit.

The coach noticed Robby standing to the side, watching the action in the pit with his helmet under his arm. Concerned, the coach asked him if he was okay, and Robby said he was. Then Coach asked him the obvious question, "Why aren't you doing the drill?"

Robby, always the thinker, said this: "First, it looks like someone could get hurt, and I don't want to get hurt. Second, I'm not sure how doing this will make me a better football player." The coach admitted to me that it was tough to argue with that logic.

I should add that Robby is now an awesome twenty-two-year-old with countless gifts to offer the world. He didn't want to play football anyway, so ultimately it didn't really matter if he participated in his fifth grade football drill or not.

However, if he *had* wanted to play, if playing football were one of his goals, then fear and uncertainty would have caused him to miss out on an opportunity that day.

He had chosen the path of least resistance, a path he could control.

―⁙―

Which brings us back to the road we travel as Christians. Most of us are great smooth-road Christians. When there is a smooth road under our feet, we are all in.

We get lulled into a false sense of security and begin to think that the road will always be smooth. We know better than that; we know there will be difficult stretches of road, but out of sight, out of mind.

Then the time will come when our faith is challenged, the road is no longer smooth: A young person dies an untimely death. A loved one is diagnosed with cancer. Our relationship with our spouse or our children is strained. There are lay-offs and budget cuts at work. There is more and more violence in our city, our country, and around the world.

We have always insisted that our faith is important to us, and it has always been a source of strength, but our faith is shaken by these difficult circumstances.

We reach the point that Matthew was writing about when Jesus said, "Whoever wishes to come after me must deny himself, take up his cross, and follow me."

We were all in when the road was smooth. When we hit a rough patch, fear and uncertainty creep in. The idea of carrying a cross is not too appealing, and the path of least resistance becomes tempting. We are literally at a crossroads.

We can take up our cross, or we can allow fear and uncertainty to get the best of us. Is our faith really worth it? What if I get hurt? How can carrying this cross possibly make me stronger?

Maybe my faith is not that important to me; maybe I can draw strength from something else or someone else. Rather than being all in, we question whether we are in at all.

When you come to that crossroads and all those questions are swirling around in your head, it may seem complicated. In the movie *God's Not Dead*, we hear these words: "Staying true to your faith isn't easy, but it is simple."

It isn't easy, but it is simple.

Either you're in or you're not. You believe or you don't. You trust or you don't. You're willing to relinquish control or you're not.

You are either part of Jesus' new marketing team or you're not.

I am not saying that we cannot ever question God's plan or have periods of doubt, but we need to wrestle with those struggles while carrying our cross.

When your faith is challenged, are you going to take up your cross and follow Him? Or are you going to stand off to the side, with your helmet under your arm?

—August 2014

How-To Instructions for Humility

Twenty-sixth Sunday in Ordinary Time 2014

Ezekiel 18:25-28
Philippian 2:1-11
Matthew 21:28-32

From the prophet Ezekiel we heard, "If he turns from the wickedness he has committed, and does what is right and just, he shall preserve his life."

From Paul's Letter to the Philippians we heard that Jesus "emptied himself, taking the form of a slave ... he humbled himself."

In the Gospel of Matthew, we heard the story of a father sending his two sons out to work in the vineyard. One son "said in reply, 'I will not,' but afterwards changed his mind" and went out and did the work.

One of the recurring themes throughout Scripture is that of humility.

In a homily delivered by Fr. Jim last year, he said that humility is the ability to look in the mirror and be honest about what we see. It is the ability to recognize our limitations and have a realistic view of who we are.

If there were a humility kit that came with how-to instructions, they might read like something like this:

Step 1: Look in the mirror and give an honest assessment.

God wants us to see our physical beauty as well as the beauty that comes from being one of His children. When we look in the mirror, He wants us to see someone who is loved, someone who has value. God wants us to embrace the gift of life He has given us and be filled with joy, awe, and wonder when we see our reflection in the mirror. If we look closely in the mirror, we will see Him standing right next to us with a smile on His face.

Finally, God wants us to be humble and honest people and acknowledge our sinfulness. Left unacknowledged, it may begin to fog up our mirrors and keep us from seeing how beautiful we really are.

Step 2: Acknowledge our sinfulness.

The *Catechism of the Catholic Church* tells us, "Sin is an offense against reason, truth, and right conscience; it is failure in genuine love for God and neighbor … it wounds the nature of man."

Even without this definition, we know what sin is, don't we? We can feel it in our gut. We know when we have done wrong. Sometimes we know right away; other times awareness comes later in the form of guilt.

We may try to soften sin by calling it "a lapse in judgment" or an "indiscretion" or "a bad habit." We may attempt to justify sin by saying something like, "I got caught up in the moment."

Step 1 in our humility kit calls us to look in the mirror and be honest. Step 2 calls us to see the good in ourselves, while acknowledging our sins, with no excuses.

Step 3: Take our sins to God and seek forgiveness.

Now that we have taken ownership of our sins, we take them to God. You might say, "God already knows. He knows everything." That is true, but bringing our sins to God is the essence of humility.

Grace comes when we speak the words, when we admit to our sins, and put ourselves at God's mercy. We must, following the example of Jesus, empty ourselves.

When talking to students about attending Mass, I used to tell them to leave their baggage at the door. I did not want the worries, distractions, and stuff of life to prevent them from experiencing the joy and miracle of the Mass.

I have changed my approach when talking to students lately. I still urge them to fully engage in the miracle of the Mass, but I talk more about transformation. Rather than leave it at the door, we should bring that baggage with us when we come to the altar to receive Holy Communion. We should offer up our fears and troubles, as well as our sins, to God. We empty ourselves, and in return, God renews us. In receiving the Body of Christ, we are transformed.

The Sacrament of Reconciliation offers us the gift of forgiveness, and we should take advantage of the opportunity to participate in the sacrament often. In the meantime, praying for God's mercy and forgiveness and bringing our sins to the altar are healthy practices as well.

Guilt and shame often keep us from seeking forgiveness. We may struggle with the same sin over and over, and we think, "How many more times will God forgive me for the same sin?" or "I don't deserve forgiveness."

Pope Francis recently said, "God never tires of forgiving us, but we sometimes tire of asking Him to forgive us."

An important note: When we seek forgiveness, let's not forget to forgive ourselves.

God expects us to follow His lead when it comes to mercy. God is well aware of our frail human nature and loves us and forgives us in spite of it.

Step 4: Do the right thing.

We took an honest look in the mirror, saw our beauty while acknowledging our sinfulness, brought our sins to God, and sought forgiveness—now what?

Simply put, we make it right. As the prophet Ezekiel said, we turn away from sin and do what is right and just.

As the son did in today's gospel, we make it right by doing the work of the Father in His vineyard.

Opening up our humility kit and following the step-by-step instructions can be very challenging. Fear is a part of any honest look in the mirror. Add to that the knowledge that we are imperfect. We know we will stumble again.

That's why there is a Step 5: repeat as necessary.

We can rejoice in the knowledge that He will never turn us away. There is nothing we could ever do to make God love us less, and His mercy knows no bounds.

After all, forgiving us is in His best interest. He wants us to be transformed so we can go about the work of bringing the gospel message to the world.

This prayer from last Friday morning's Liturgy of the Hours says it well:

Father, he who knew no sin was made sin for us, to save us and restore us to Your friendship. Look upon our contrite heart and afflicted spirit and heal our troubled conscience, so that with the joy and strength of the Holy Spirit we may proclaim your praise and glory before all the nations. Amen.

—September 2014

THE SMELL OF THE SHEEP

Solemnity of Christ   *Ezekiel 34:11-12, 15-17*
the King 2014   *1 Corinthians 15:20-26, 28*
                             Matthew 25:31-46

When the kids were little, Carol used to make their Halloween costumes. When our oldest daughter, Mary, was four years old, she wanted to be a sheep. So Carol made a costume and turned her into an adorable little sheep.

The next year, we attempted to pass the costume on to three-year-old Rick. He refused. The reason he gave: "Sheep are stinky."

I don't know exactly how he came to that conclusion—we did not live on a farm, and he had not traveled extensively in his three years.

Regardless, sheep do stink, so we could not argue with him. Carol made some horns that she attached to the headpiece of the costume, and he seemed quite content to go trick-or-treating as a ram.

I know, rams are sheep. But Rick didn't know that.

A tie-in to smelly sheep will come later in the homily.

Growing up, two of my siblings, Sharon and Mark, used to work at an Arby's Restaurant. When they came home from work, they smelled like Arby's. Their clothes, their hair, and their car smelled like roast beef, with just a hint of sesame seeds.

I'm not complaining; I liked Arby's. I'm just saying that they smelled like their work.

A tie-in to smelling like your work will come later in the homily.

⸻

Today we celebrate the Feast of Christ the King. What is our image of Christ the King?

At the beginning of today's gospel reading, we are presented with this image:

"When the Son of Man comes in his glory, and all the angels with him, he will sit upon his glorious throne, and all the nations will be assembled before him."

As the gospel goes on, that image quickly changes, however. Christ the King transforms. He becomes a shepherd, separating sheep from goats.

That is the king *we* know, the God with whom *we* feel comfortable. Our king is the Good Shepherd.

The first reading from Ezekiel paints a beautiful picture of the Good Shepherd: "I myself will look after and tend my sheep ... The lost I will seek out ... the strayed I will bring back, the injured I will bind up, the sick I will heal."

A king sits on a throne overlooking his kingdom, looking down upon his subjects. The Good Shepherd is out among his sheep, side by side, up close and personal.

In March of 2013, Pope Francis encouraged the world's bishops to bring the healing power of God's grace to everyone in need, to stay close to the marginalized and to be "shepherds living with the smell of the sheep."

Basically, the Good Shepherd smells like His sheep. He smells like His work.

Jesus did not sit at the seat of honor at a banquet. He did not accumulate wealth or rub elbows with the rich. He did not dress to impress.

Jesus spent his time with the poor. He walked among the lepers. He connected with people on the fringe by going out and living on the fringe. He washed feet. Jesus rolled up his sleeves and got to work.

He understood His sheep because He was with them every day. "I know my sheep and My sheep know Me."

He lived with the smell of the sheep.

In today's gospel, Jesus makes it very clear that He expects us to follow His lead: He expects us to give food to the hungry and drink to those who thirst. He expects us to welcome strangers and clothe the naked. He expects us to care for the sick and visit the imprisoned. These are the actions that allow us to inherit the kingdom.

Many of you know that I work with an organization called HOOP. We bring food, blankets, and other necessities to the homeless living under bridges or in makeshift shelters along the White River.

However, we do more than that. We talk to them. We provide human contact and assurance that they are not forgotten.

I try not to eat very much on the days I will be going out with HOOP. I want to feel the hunger pangs of those I serve, even if just for a few hours. I don't shower right away after coming home. I don't want to warm up, knowing that the homeless won't be warm at all that night. I sit in my coat for a short time. I want to smell the campfire smoke that has permeated the coat. I want to remember that fire is the only source of heat for the homeless while I sit in my house with the thermostat set at a comfortable seventy degrees.

I need to, in small ways, experience some of what the homeless experience every day. I need to smell like the sheep for a few moments.

Jesus wants us to be smelly. He wants us in the trenches. Hungry, vulnerable people are all around us.

"For I was hungry, and you gave me food. "

All people need to be fed. Food is more than soup and a sandwich. We feed people by treating them with respect. We feed them when we lift them up and affirm them. We feed others when we show love and compassion. We feed their spirit.

"I was a stranger and you welcomed me, naked and you clothed me."

Anyone can feel like a stranger or feel naked and vulnerable. We can clothe them with dignity. We can offer a smile and a handshake and human interaction. We can look them in the eye rather than quickly looking away to avoid contact.

"I was in prison and you visited me. "

Not all prisons have bars. Many people are imprisoned by the circumstances of their lives. Poverty, depression, addiction, loneliness— each prisons in its own way. We visit the imprisoned when we reach out to them. When we pick up the phone or drop them a note or meet them for coffee. We visit them when we listen. Our visit says to them, "You are important." Our visit may be the key that unlocks their prison cell.

When we do all of these things, we are in the trenches—up close and personal.

We are, as Pope Francis says, "living with the smell of the sheep."

When we arrive at heaven's gate, maybe we will be judged by how long our list of good deeds is. Or, maybe, we will be judged by how we smell.

—November 2014

FIGHT FOR FRONT ROW SEATS

Solemnity of the Most Holy Body   *Exodus 24:3-8*
and Blood of Christ 2015   *Hebrews 9:11-15*
      Mark 14:12-16, 22-26

During my freshmen year of college, it was announced that Billy Joel would be coming to campus to perform. To those who do not know who Billy Joel is, he is, in my humble opinion, the greatest musical artist of all time. I was, and obviously still am, a big Billy Joel fan, so there was no doubt that I was going to do whatever it took to get tickets.

The promoters announced that tickets would go on sale beginning at 10:00 a.m. the following Tuesday morning, and that students would be allowed to line up to buy tickets beginning at 12:00 noon on Monday. I was at the arena, with my lawn chair, at 12:00 noon on Monday. I am happy to report I was the eleventh person in line.

In order to execute this twenty-two-hour vigil, I needed to miss two classes on Monday afternoon and another on Tuesday morning. As an educator, I am certainly not condoning my behavior, but it was, after all, Billy Joel. This type of decision-making may explain why it took me five and a half years to get my four-year college degree.

Missing classes and sleeping in a lawn chair were worth it. I would have done anything to get front row tickets to see Billy Joel.

Who is *your* Billy Joel? What musical group, top athlete, movie star, or mega-celebrity causes your heart to race? Who would you stand in line for hours to see? Or fight for a front row seat?

Maybe for you it's Pope Francis. We have seen pictures that show hundreds of thousands of people packing the streets just to get a glimpse of the Pope.

We all love Fr. Jim and Fr. John, but what if we announced that Pope Francis would be here to celebrate Mass at St. Pius X next weekend? People would start lining up immediately. At that Mass, the front rows would be taken first. We would have to hire security to keep order.

Fr. Jim, we could even charge admission and close that parish financial gap you've been taking about.

What does all of this have to do with our celebration of the Most Holy Body and Blood of Christ? It points out the irony of the situation.

The biggest mega-celebrity of all-time, Jesus Christ Himself, is present at every Mass we celebrate. He is truly present. The Real Presence of Christ, in our midst each time we celebrate Mass. Why are there no lines to get in?

The community brings forward the gifts of bread and wine. Moments later, the priest offers the words of consecration, and transubstantiation takes place.

What is transubstantiation? In the act of consecration during the Eucharistic prayer, the substance of the bread and wine is changed by the power of the Holy Spirit into the substance of the Body and Blood of Jesus Christ. At the same time, the appearance and taste of the bread and wine remain the same.

Thus in the Eucharist, the bread ceases to be bread in substance and becomes the Body of Christ while the wine ceases to be wine in substance and becomes the Blood of Christ.

The Institution of the Eucharist, the words spoken by Jesus at the Last Supper, comes to life in today's gospel: "He took bread, said the blessing, broke it, gave it to them, and said, 'Take it; this is my body.' Then he took a cup, gave thanks, and gave it to them. He said to them, 'This is my blood.'"

The Real Presence of Christ, in our midst each time we celebrate Mass. A miracle takes place at every Mass, yet there is no fanfare. There are no long lines to get into church. There are no fights for front row seats.

Why is that? Because many Catholics don't believe in the Real Presence, and most of us have doubts.

The Catholic Church is rich in symbols. A server processes in with a crucifix. It symbolizes Jesus sacrificing His life for us by His death on the cross. It's not really Jesus on that cross. It is a symbol.

We have the risen Christ hanging in the front of the church. It symbolizes the hope of the resurrection. It is not really the risen Christ. It is a symbol.

Candles, statues, icons—all symbols.

The Eucharist is *not* a symbol. It is the Real Presence of Christ. It is difficult to wrap our minds around that concept, so we doubt.

Here is something to keep in mind: when it comes to our faith, doubt is acceptable.

Comprehending concepts such as Real Presence, the Trinity, heaven, or even God's unfailing love for us can be a monumental task. That is why the Church uses the word *mystery* to refer to something that escapes the full comprehension of the human mind. Isn't that the essence of faith? Belief in something we cannot fully understand? Something we cannot explain or prove empirically?

Doubt is okay. It is a very human response. The key is in how we address our doubt. The easy path is to simply reject what we don't understand. I don't understand it, I can't explain it, I can't prove it, so I reject it. Therefore, I reject the Church. That is the path chosen by so many who have left the church.

Here's another option: Why not put our doubt to work? What if our doubt led us to dig deeper, to ask questions, to explore the teachings of the Church? What if we totally immersed ourselves in the miracle of the Mass? What if we spent time praying about those things we do not fully comprehend? We could also pray for the courage to trust, to accept that there are things bigger than ourselves that we will never truly understand.

In Matthew's gospel last weekend, the risen Christ appeared to the eleven apostles in Galilee. The gospel read, "When the disciples saw him, they worshipped, but they doubted." The men chosen by Jesus to build the Church doubted. However, it is important to note that while experiencing their doubt, they continued to worship.

Permission to doubt has been granted to us. However, the call to worship remains. We worship not in spite of our doubt but in harmony with it.

Prepare yourselves—the Real Presence of Christ will soon be in our midst.

Get in line and fight for that front row seat; then put your doubt to work.

— June 2015

FINDING THE PARKING SPACE

Fourteenth Sunday in
Ordinary Time 2015

Ezekiel 2:2-5
2 Corinthians 12:7-10
Mark 6:1-6

Back when Lou Holtz was the head football coach at Notre Dame, he and his wife were out to dinner in Miami a few nights before his team was to play in the Orange Bowl. A waiter came to him and asked, "You're Coach Holtz from Notre Dame, aren't you?"

Assuming the young man wanted an autograph, he reached into his pocket for a pen and replied, "Yes, I am."

"In that case," the waiter said. "I have a question for you: what's the difference between Cheerios and Notre Dame?"

"I have no idea," Coach Holtz replied.

The waiter said, "Cheerios belong in a bowl, and Notre Dame doesn't."

Coach Holtz fumed the entire dinner. When the same waiter brought him his check at the end of the meal, Holtz said, "By the way, I have a question for you: what's the difference between golf pros and Lou Holtz?"

"I have no idea," the waiter replied.

Holtz said, "Golf pros give tips."

Sorry, that has nothing to do with my homily.

I just thought it was funny.

In May, Coach Holtz was the commencement speaker for Franciscan University of Steubenville. His speech was laced with one-liners and stories, but in the midst of the humor was a beautiful message of doing the right thing and trusting God.

One story he shared was this: A man was late for a business meeting. He was driving through a parking lot, searching frantically for an open parking space. After driving the entire lot multiple times and finding none, he was exasperated.

He tried to make a deal with God. Looking up to heaven, he said. "God, if you open up a parking spot for me, I will go to church every Sunday, pray the Rosary each night, and treat everyone I meet with love."

After he finished speaking, there was a loud clap of thunder, and a parking space miraculously opened up right in front of him.

Elated, he looked up to God and said, "Never mind, I found one myself."

Human beings are slow to ask for help and quick to claim the credit.

Today's readings are about strength, power, weakness, and vulnerability—and the irony that ties them all together. Most people equate strength and power with rugged individualism. A person who is strong physically and mentally is one who has an inner resolve, a discipline that allows him to be in control and deal with whatever may come his way, on his own terms. I am strong because I am in control, and control equals power. We envision ourselves as superheroes, with bullets bouncing off our chests.

There is merit in *some* of this line of thought. It is good to have resolve. It is good to work hard to handle all that life throws at us and to be mentally and physically sharp. It is good to be prepared for challenges that are sure to come.

Where we are misguided is in our belief that we are superheroes, that we are in control and can do it all alone. We consider depending on anyone other than ourselves to be a sign of weakness.

This line of thought seems to be with us from early on in our lives. Have you ever tried to help young children do something for the first time? "I can do it myself!" they will tell you.

Ironically, it is this very perception of strength and power that makes us vulnerable. If we're in control, where does God fit in?

———

What did St. Paul mean when he wrote, "When I am weak, then I am strong"?

When our lives are running smoothly, devoid of difficulties or challenges, it is easy to rely only on oneself. However, when we face the storms that ultimately come, we find that we are not strong enough to handle them on our own. Rather than reach out for help, we stubbornly do it alone. Our pride gets in the way. We live by the philosophy of "never let 'em see you sweat."

To admit that we can't do it on our own is to admit weakness. So we flounder and sink deeper into life's difficulties.

In these times of personal struggles, we must acknowledge our weakness and turn to God. We can rely on Him and His strength to carry us through the storm. When we accept that we are not in control and turn to God, in our weakness we are made strong. When facing hardship and adversity, our willingness to reach out to God and our faith that He can help us make us strong.

It is what allowed St. Paul to write, "Therefore, I am content with weaknesses, insults, hardships, persecutions, and constraints. "

His faith allowed for that contentment and acceptance. As Paul wrote in that same letter, "God's grace is sufficient for me."

———

If we are indeed superheroes, then thinking that we are in control is our kryptonite. Kryptonite is the one thing that makes Superman vulnerable. As a superhero, he has many strengths, many superpowers: he is faster than a speeding bullet, more powerful than a locomotive, and able to leap tall buildings in a single bound.

Yet kryptonite, a green radioactive rock, can drain his power and leave him vulnerable. Every superhero has his own kryptonite, something that drains him of his power.

In today's gospel, we learn that Jesus had a kryptonite too. Mark tells us that Jesus was, "not able to perform any mighty deed" while in his native place.

This was due to the lack of faith of the people living there. *Their* lack of faith was *His* kryptonite.

Because the people in his native place thought they were in control, because they did not have faith in His ability to help them, Jesus was powerless.

Our kryptonite is the belief that we are in control. It drains us and makes us vulnerable. It also shows a lack of faith, which in turn, leaves Jesus powerless to help us.

So what's the answer? We must redefine what it means to be strong. Being strong has nothing to do with being in control and everything to do with being self-aware.

Being prepared to take on life's challenges, striving to be self-reliant, and providing support for others in their time of need are all a part of what it means to be strong.

However, true strength lies in acknowledging our limitations and embracing our weakness. When we acknowledge our weakness and seek help, then we are strong.

We must recognize that we are not in control. When we do that and put our faith in God, we no longer hinder Him, allowing His power to flow through us. True strength lies in recognizing that we need God's help and then believing in and accepting that help.

True strength lies in understanding that we can't always find the parking space on our own.

—July 2015

144 PENS

Twentieth Sunday in Ordinary Time 2015　*Proverbs 9:1-6*
Ephesians 5:15-20
John 6:51-58

Four weeks ago, we heard the story of the miracle of the multiplication of the loaves and fishes. For the last three weeks, we have been reading what is referred to as the Bread of Life Discourse, found in John's Gospel, chapter 6, verses 22–58.

So for a month, we have been hearing about bread and being fed:

- "Bread from heaven"
- "I am the bread of life"
- "Whoever eats this bread will live forever"
- "The one who feeds on me will have life"
- "Feed them yourselves"
- "All ate and were satisfied"

After four weeks of gospels about bread, eating, and feeding others, what else can possibly be said? I couldn't think of anything, so I have decided to talk instead about my favorite pen.

Not too many people here know this about me, but I can get pretty set in my ways. I like what I like. I get comfortable with certain things.

When I was principal at Guerin Catholic, my assistant, Cathy, took care of purchasing all the office supplies needed at the school. So she would purchase pens as I needed them. About four years ago, she dropped a package of pens, a three-pack, on my desk.

When I opened the package for the first time and held one of the pens in my hand, I knew—it was perfect. The cushioned grip fit my hand perfectly. The ink flowed smoothly from its fine point. It was sleek and efficient.

I looked for excuses to write things down. I waited anxiously for people to come to my office to ask me to sign something.

This was to be my pen. From that day forward, I would accept no substitutes.

However, the day came when Cathy set a different pen down on my desk. She reported that the hook at the store was empty and that this particular pen, my pen, had been discontinued. She could see the pained look on my face as I stared with disdain at this *other* pen she brought me. She promised to try some other stores, which she did, but to no avail. The store manager looked up the pen and confirmed that the manufacturer was no longer making that pen.

Not to be denied, I took the search to the Internet. After being turned down at numerous sites, I came across one vendor that claimed to have some in stock.

I called them and asked them to confirm that they had my pen.

"How many do you want?" they asked.

"How many do you *have*?" I replied.

"We have 144 in stock," they said.

I know what you're thinking. Yes, I did. I purchased 144 pens that day. I will never have to write with another type of pen for as long as I live.

I like what I like. I'm set in my ways. I want to be comfortable.

There are a few other things. If I find a shirt that is particularly comfortable, I'll buy the same shirt in six different colors. Comfortable shoes? I'll buy three pair at a time, maybe four.

Now, when we're talking about things like pens and shirts and shoes, we can get away with being set in our ways and being focused only on our own need to be comfortable. However, there is a danger in taking that same philosophy into our daily interactions with others or allowing it to impact our ability to accept others for who they are.

But there are some people who make us uncomfortable, aren't there? They may have a different faith or value system. They may be a different race or speak a different language. They may be in a different income bracket or travel in different social circles.

Maybe older people or teenagers make us uncomfortable. Perhaps the homeless or addicts. Maybe someone has hurt us or a former friend seems to be drifting further and further away. We stay hurt and ignore the drifting apart because initiating reconciliation takes us out of our comfort zone.

Being set in our ways and avoiding situations and people that make us uncomfortable may be easier, but it is not what Jesus calls us to do.

In today's second reading, St. Paul wrote to the Ephesians: "Do not continue in ignorance, but try to understand what is the will of the Lord."

To discover His will, we return to what Jesus said to his disciples when five thousand hungry people sat before Him with nothing to eat: "Feed them yourselves."

After the multiplication of the loaves and fishes, the people were fed, and we are told, "*All* ate and were satisfied."

Again, "*All* ate and were satisfied."

Jesus didn't feed half of the five thousand or *most* of the people. He fed them *all*. He didn't walk among them, saying, "You can eat, but you cannot" or "You will be fed, and you will not."

They *all* ate and were satisfied. We are called to nourish everyone we meet, not just those with whom we feel comfortable.

A great example of this is my wife's recent trip to Tanzania. When she returned from the trip, I watched a video of Carol teaching an art lesson to students in Tanzania.

Carol, a fifty-something-year-old white American female who speaks absolutely no Swahili, teaching a group of forty black fifteen-year-old Tanzanian males the art of origami. For those who are not familiar with origami, it is a *Japanese* art form. And no, she doesn't speak Japanese either.

Carol was smiling and laughing as she spoke with her hands and her facial expressions; they were smiling and laughing along with her. They were all nourished, including Carol. All ate and were satisfied.

In order to feed others, we must explore and embrace our differences. Church cannot be defined by the limitations of this building.

That's what the Bread of Life Discourse is all about. We turn to Jesus, the Bread of Life, for nourishment, but that is only the first step. We must then feed others. All must be fed.

So go ahead and hoard your favorite pen and buy six identical shirts if that makes you comfortable. However, carrying out "the will of the Lord" dictates that we move outside of our comfort zone.

Pope Francis told us recently that if we are truly to make disciples of all men, we must "stop fishing in our own aquarium."

—August 2015

DIAL IN TO GOD'S FREQUENCY

Twenty-third Sunday in Ordinary Time 2015   *Isaiah 35:4-7*
James 2:1-5
Mark 7:31-37

One of my prior jobs was that of high school athletic director. There were many details to the job, most of which revolved around the logistics of game night: contracting the opponent, hiring officials, overseeing ticket sales, providing for fan safety, supervising the behavior of fans, and so on.

An interesting, and somewhat sad, result of being an athletic director was that I found it very difficult to enjoy sports in my free time. I would go to a college game, or even a Colts or Pacers game, and experience anxiety.

If I saw someone slip and fall, I would worry about a lawsuit. If I saw long lines at the concession stand, I would have concerns about customer satisfaction. I would have the urge to correct the behavior of unruly fans.

If I didn't see enough game officials, I would think, "Oh no! What if one of them didn't show up?"

I could not turn off the noise of my job long enough to enjoy time away from the job.

The other day at school, the administration watched a newly completed promotional video that highlighted the everyday life of the school. It showed students at various times throughout their day—walking the halls and sharing a laugh with a friend, discussing something with a teacher, working out a problem at the whiteboard, or giving a presentation in front of the class.

Music accompanied the video, adding an even more positive and uplifting vibe to it. No one could possibly watch that video and not feel good about our school.

I turned to one of the assistant principals, who is in charge of school safety and discipline, and asked, "What did you think about the video?"

He replied, "All I saw were uniform violations."

His single-minded focus prevented him from really experiencing the video.

Along these same lines, I want to spend some time reflecting on our ability to focus, looking specifically at the phenomenon of *selective hearing.*

In analyzing selective hearing, we learn that it can be defined in two different ways. As a specialized skill, selective hearing can be used to filter out the white noise of the world and focus in on one particular sound.

One example would be the mother at a noisy dinner party who is able to hear her infant cry out from a room in another part of the house. I once heard that described as a mother and child being "on the same frequency." She was dialed in; she selected what is most important to hear and chose not to be distracted by anything that would prevent her from hearing it.

Selective hearing may also be used as a tool of *convenience*. Those adept at this particular form of selective hearing are able to filter out anything that is inconsistent with what they *want* to hear.

My wife would claim that husbands are quite proficient at this, but I will offer children as my example. You tell your son he can go outside as soon as he cleans his room. Later, you see him outside and, upon inspection, discover he has not yet cleaned his room. When you confront him about this, he will swear that you never said anything about cleaning his room. He heard "play outside" but did not hear "clean your room."

We select what we *want* to hear and *filter out* words that challenge us or do not meet our needs.

I remember seeing a comic strip once that showed a man putting in his new hearing aid. He said, "It's called a selective hearing aid. It filters out criticism and amplifies compliments."

Both types of selective hearing I mentioned rely on the ability to filter out unwanted noise or information.

What keeps us from hearing God's word? Are we unable to filter properly and thus distracted by the noise of the world? Or are we simply *filtering out* what God has to say because we find it too challenging?

In Mark's gospel, we heard the Aramaic word *ephphetha*, which we are told means, "be opened." Jesus said this word as He touched the ears and tongue of a man, enabling him to hear and speak for the first time.

During a baptism, there is an optional part of the ceremony called the Ephphetha Rite. In this rite, the celebrant touches the ears and lips of the child with his thumb, saying: "The Lord Jesus made the deaf hear and the dumb speak. May God touch your ears to receive His word and your mouth to proclaim his faith to the praise and glory of God the Father."

"May God soon touch your ears to receive His word."

He wants us to hear Him.

Today's first reading had the same message. The prophet Isaiah told us, "Your God comes to save you … the ears of the deaf be cleared."

God desires to be heard, to be the infant in the other room at the dinner party. He wants us to filter out the noise of the world and focus on Him. He wants us to be on the same frequency. Why? Because each time God speaks, there is an opportunity to grow.

That's why Jesus often ended His parables by saying, "Whoever has ears ought to hear."

How do we master the specialized skill of selective hearing, the type that allows us to filter out the noise of the world and focus on what's most important?

Here are a few suggestions:

- Make yourself available to God. The reason the world has our attention is because we make ourselves available to the world. We spend our days interacting with, thinking about, and reflecting on the things of this world. We must notch out a piece of our day to give to God. The world gets enough of our time.
- Make morning prayer nonnegotiable. Breakfast is the most important meal of the day, and morning prayer is the most important prayer of the day. It tells God, "*You* come first. This day is for *You*."
- Spend time with Scripture. It is the divinely inspired word of God. He talks to us through scripture, and the message is personalized—each person hears what God intends him or her to hear.

How will *you* use selective hearing? Will you filter out what God has to say because you find it too challenging, allowing the distractions of the world to garner all your attention?

Or will you filter out the noise of the world and focus in on what God has to say to you?

We *love* when we *listen*.

"May God touch your ears to receive His word."

He may touch your *ears*, but the transmitter is in your *heart*. Tune out the noise of the world and dial in to God's frequency.

—September 2015

God Doesn't Need
Autocorrect

Twenty-seventh Sunday in
Ordinary Time 2015

Genesis 2:18-24
Hebrews 2:9-11
Mark 10:2-12

I would like to share a few thoughts on the Autocorrect feature on my phone. For those who may be unfamiliar with Autocorrect, allow me to explain. The role of this electronic feature, in theory, is to alert you when you have made an error while typing a text and display for you the most likely choice for what you *meant* to say.

It seems quite capable of catching *minor* errors. For example, I typed capital *I* and lowercase *m* at the beginning of a sentence, leaving out the apostrophe. Autocorrect alerted me and offered, "*I*-apostrophe-*m*" as an alternative. If I accept that alternative, I simply keep typing, and it will automatically make the change for me. Thanks, Autocorrect!

In reality, the majority of the time that Autocorrect has attempted to "help" me, it has simply offered a different error than the one I made myself.

Another example: In my haste to type the word *because,* I mixed up the order of several letters. Autocorrect was on the job, so it offered me the alternative: *bacon slice.*

No, Autocorrect, in my correspondence with Fr. Jim about weekend Masses, I did not intend to write *bacon slice*.

Generally what happens is that you are typing so quickly and hitting Send that many text messages are sent out with new ridiculous errors instead of the simple ones you made on your own.

Case in point: Carol took some students to Washington, DC, to see Pope Francis. She arrived home at two o'clock last Friday morning. The car she had rented for the trip needed to be returned by noon, so she wanted me to call her at eleven in the morning to make sure she was awake.

I called her at 11:00. No answer.

I called her every ten minutes after that. No answer.

Finally, at 12:15, I received a text from Carol. What she *intended* to text to me was "I'm awake. Need keys to get in the house."

Instead, the message she sent said, "I'm awake. Need keys. Tiger in the house."

Well, that certainly explained why Carol wasn't answering her phone. A tiger in the house can keep a person pretty busy.

So what's the connection?

Through His Son, Jesus, God sent us His message of unconditional love for all. That message resonates this weekend as the Archdiocese celebrates Respect Life Sunday.

St. John Paul II once said, "The deepest element of God's commandment is the requirement to show reverence and love for every person and the life of every person."

Respecting life means offering love and acceptance to all. However, over the years it seems we have taken it upon ourselves to act as God's autocorrect. We often change His message to something He never intended, perhaps to make it more manageable.

We respect life, so we are entrenched in the battle against abortion. Do we also love, pray for, and welcome women who have, for whatever reason, made the decision to have an abortion? If *not*, aren't we taking it upon ourselves to change God's message?

We respect life, so we take time to visit the imprisoned; but acting as God's autocorrect, we determine that *others* in prison are deserving of the death penalty. When we advocate for that, aren't we taking it upon ourselves to change God's message?

Respecting life means offering love and acceptance to all.

We donate money to the poor, but are we comfortable making eye contact with them or inviting them into our home?

We respect all life, so we know that the elderly deserve our love and attention, but we're just so busy.

Respecting life means offering love and acceptance to all.

We can even use the strong message Jesus shared about marriage as an example. Throughout the gospels, including today's reading from Luke, Jesus presented a certain vision for human relationships, including within marriage. However, He never condemned those who fell short of that vision.

Divorce does not make either party in the broken marriage less valuable, or less worthy of dignity and respect. Thanks to Pope Francis, the Church has made it clear that divorced Catholics "are not to be treated as second class citizens."

Respecting life means offering love and acceptance to all.

As for myself, I support marriage, I prepare couples for marriage, and I preach about marriage, yet I know I often take my *own* marriage for granted.

Who am I to act as God's autocorrect?

Starting tomorrow, bishops from around the world will be gathering to discuss ways to promote and support healthy family life. The bishops will *not* be attempting to correct God's message of unconditional love. We all know of family units that are dysfunctional or have disintegrated and still others that are nontraditional in their makeup. Members of those families will not be deemed less valuable by the bishops or less worthy of love and respect. They too fall under the banner of "reverence and love for every person."

In my role as a school administrator and deacon, I have often spoken about and written about what is needed to ensure a strong family unit, yet I have often fallen short as a father myself.

Who am I to act as God's autocorrect?

As followers of Jesus Christ, we are forever in pursuit of the elusive ideals with which He has challenged us. We do our best, we stumble and fall, and we start over, hoping one day to fully embrace the vision Jesus has for us.

In spite of our struggles, God loves us unconditionally. He never wavers from His simple message of love for every person.

Others around us will stumble and fall and will need to start over in their hope of attaining the vision Jesus has for them. If we truly respect life, we will love them all.

We do not need to support, promote, or condone all human behavior, but we *are* called to love and accept all human beings. God calls us to show reverence and love for every person and the life of every person.

His message is just fine as it is; God doesn't need autocorrect.

—October 2015

RELENTLESS

Thirtieth Sunday in Ordinary Time 2015   ***Jeremiah 31:7-9***
Hebrews 5:1-6
Mark 10:46-52

While delivering homilies, I have sometimes shared stories involving members of my family. People will often ask me, "Does your family mind that you talk about them like that?" We have talked about it as a family, and they don't seem to mind.

I have something to include in my homily today that my wife may prefer that I *not* share. However, I put Carol on a plane to El Salvador on Wednesday morning. With her safely out of the country, I'm going for it.

I'm sure that when people see my beautiful wife and I together, they wonder to themselves, "How did he end up with her?"

They assume I must have money or that it was an arranged marriage. Those assumptions don't hurt my feelings. I am well aware of the fact that I married way out of my league.

So what is my secret? Persistence.

The first time I asked Carol to marry me, she said, "No." Now, if Carol were here, she'd say, "Well ... I didn't really say no."

I was there. I know a no when I hear it. But I didn't take no for an answer. I was a squeaky wheel. I was persistent. I was a step above persistent. I was relentless.

Two months later, she said, "Yes."

<hr>

Last year, I had a student who said she really wanted one of our school rules changed. She made an appointment, came to my office, and made her case for the change. She was polite, but not well-informed, and seemed to know it was a lost cause before she ever began.

I listened attentively, acknowledged her effort, and explained why the rule was in place. I also explained why it would not be changed.

For the next couple of months, she came to my office about once a week to restate her case and ask me to reconsider changing the rule. There was no passion in her voice. It seemed she was really just killing time.

Eventually, I grew tired of her dropping in to my office. Doing my best not to offend her or hurt her feelings, I said, "You know, *some people* might consider all of these trips to my office kind of annoying."

She seemed caught off guard by my comment, and said innocently, "I'm so sorry, I didn't mean to be annoying. I was trying to be persistent."

<hr>

I saw a comic strip once that showed a man talking to his boss. You could see his fellow employees in the background, carrying picket signs demanding higher wages. The man told his boss, "You have to give in before too long. The squeaky wheel gets the grease, you know."

In the second panel, the boss responded, "Not necessarily. Sometimes the squeaky wheel gets replaced."

Which leads us to some questions: When are we being annoying and when are we being persistent? When is being a squeaky wheel a good thing, and when is it a bad thing?

—◦◦◦◦—

In today's gospel, we meet Bartimaeus. He was blind, likely from birth and resorted to begging due to his condition. Some found him annoying. After calling out to Jesus, we are told that "many rebuked him, telling him to be silent."

I am sure they were thinking to themselves, "Who does this beggar think he is, bothering a man as important as Jesus?"

He was definitely a squeaky wheel. Mark tells us that Bartimaeus "kept calling out all the more, 'Son of David, have pity on me.'"

Yet *Jesus* considered him persistent and rewarded him for it.

What was it about Bartimaeus that moved Jesus to give him his sight and say, "Your faith has saved you"?

There are a few things that Jesus recognized in this blind beggar that others did not:

First, Bartimaeus believed. He believed Jesus was capable of giving him his sight. It is likely that he had heard of Jesus healing others. As Jesus traveled, word about the miraculous healings He had performed spread. Now, throngs of people followed Him wherever he went. Bartimaeus heard about Jesus and believed. Without seeing it with his own eyes—*unable* to see it with his own eyes—he believed. He had absolute faith in Jesus. Happy are those who have not seen, and yet believe.

Second, Bartimaeus took action. Jesus might never pass that way again. He knew that if he were going to receive help, then he needed to act when he had the chance. The gospel tells us that when Jesus responded to him, Bartimaeus "threw aside his cloak, sprang up, and came to Jesus."

This blind man had a desire, and he ran to Jesus with that desire. If he had not acted right then, he would have been blind forever. *It was his faith that allowed him to take action.*

Third, Bartimaeus spoke with confidence. Jesus said to him, "What do you want me to do for you?"

Bartimaeus replied, "Master, I want to see."

He did not say, "I hope you can do this" or "Could you try to give me my sight?"

He simply stated his desire to Jesus: "I want to see." *It was his faith that allowed him to speak with confidence.*

Finally, Bartimaeus followed through. Throughout Scripture, we read about others who were healed. Often they run away to spread the news to their family and friends. Some simply disappear without even a thank-you.

Not Bartimaeus.

Jesus even opened the door for him to walk away, saying, "Go your way; your faith has saved you."

However, he saw that Christ's way was a far better way than his own. The gospel tells us, "Immediately he received his sight and followed Jesus on the way."

It was his faith that allowed him to follow through.

Bartimaeus was not annoying. He was not an irritating squeaky wheel, but a persistent one. His faith allowed him to take action, to speak confidently, and to follow through. His faith allowed him to be relentless.

Jesus wants our own faith to give us the courage to do the same. He wants us to pursue Him relentlessly.

Even a blind man can see that.

—October 2015

ABOUT THE AUTHOR

Deacon Rick Wagner was ordained a permanent deacon in 2012 and is currently assigned to St. Pius X Parish in Indianapolis, IN. In addition to his responsibilities at the parish, he serves as principal and vice president of mission and ministry at Bishop Chatard High School, also in Indianapolis.

Prior to his role at Bishop Chatard, Deacon Rick served as principal of Guerin Catholic High School in Noblesville, Indiana. Before beginning his tenure at Guerin Catholic, he served as director of Our Lady of Fatima Retreat House in Indianapolis.

His first book, *Remember What's Important*, was published in 2011.

Deacon Rick has been married to his wife, Carol, for thirty-three years. They have four children and six grandchildren.

CPSIA information can be obtained
at www.ICGtesting.com
Printed in the USA
LVOW11s1556041216

515740LV00001B/83/P